A Life
in ЯED

John F. Blair, Publisher
Winston-Salem, North Carolina

A Life
in ЯED

*A Story of Forbidden Love,
the Great Depression,
and the Communist Fight
for a Black Nation
in the Deep South*

David Beasley

JOHN F. BLAIR,
P U B L I S H E R
1406 Plaza Drive
Winston-Salem, North Carolina 27103
www.blairpub.com

Library of Congress Cataloging-in-Publication Data

Beasley, David, 1958-
  A life in red : a story of forbidden love, the Great Depression, and the communist fight for a Black nation in the deep South / by David Beasley.
       pages   cm
   Includes bibliographical references and index.
  ISBN 978-0-89587-622-5 (alkaline paper) — ISBN 978-0-89587-623-2 (ebook) 1. Newton, Herbert. 2. Newton, Jane Emery. 3. African American communists—Southern States—Biography. 4. Women communists—Southern States—Biography. 5. Interracial marriage—Southern States--History—20th century. 6. African Americans—Civil rights—Southern States—History—20th century. 7. National liberation movements—Southern States—History—20th century. 8. Communism—Southern States—History—20th century. 9. Depressions—1929—Southern States. 10. Southern States—Race relations—History—20th century. I. Title.
  HX84.N49B43 2015
  335.43092′275—dc23
  [B]
                                        2015018196

10 9 8 7 6 5 4 3 2 1

To my wife, Susan

CONTENTS

Peace, thou child of scarlet
That always goes in black.
What is the color in your heart
To that upon your back?

If you would wear a red gown,
Waste no time being old;
Black is for the wise ones,
Crimson for the bold.

Jane Newton

PROLOGUE

The French Scholar wrote Jane Newton for the first time on January 2, 1963, rekindling old memories.

Michel Fabre, a graduate student teaching for a year at Harvard, wrote from the cold confines of Cambridge, Massachusetts. Jane was still living in Brooklyn but later that year would move to sunny Santa Barbara, California, nestled on the Pacific Coast, where the winters were mild and refreshing.

She would become the city clerk of Santa Barbara, a resort town nicknamed "the American Riviera." Here, the citizens enjoyed three hundred days of sunshine every year and only fifteen inches of rainfall. Each morning, mist from the sea lifted and the town slowly came to life to the sound of sea gulls and the smell of the Pacific Ocean.

Jane would be out of her element in this land of sunshine and palm trees. Fabre's letter brought her back to the cold, gray 1930s. He was working on a doctoral thesis about the African American novelist Richard Wright and asked Jane for help, knowing that she and her husband, Herbert

Newton, had been close to Wright when they were all members of the American Communist Party.

The Newtons' marriage was radical in many ways. Jane was white, the daughter of the former head of the American Legion, the symbol of American patriotism. Herbert Newton was black, Boston-born and Moscow-trained, a career Communist agitator who tried to persuade African Americans in the American South to launch an uprising, even to form their own separate nation.

Jane and Herbert eventually attracted national attention, along with the fear and ire of the Ku Klux Klan, for what they represented and what it portended: a wicked combination of interracial marriage and Communism.

Also in the mix was Wright, born in the Mississippi Delta, grandson of slaves, possessor of only an eighth-grade education, who fell under the spell of the Communist movement. Wright died in 1960 in Paris at age fifty-two, having lived his last years in bitter, self-imposed exile from the United States, forever wounded, forever repulsed by the racism he had experienced there.

While living with Jane and Herbert Newton in Brooklyn, Wright wrote his most successful novel, *Native Son*. Published in 1940, the novel portrayed a black murderer in Chicago named Bigger Thomas, a man provoked to violence by racism, by the "crime of being black."[1]

Wright sought no sympathy for Bigger Thomas, who murdered a wealthy, Communist white woman and stuffed her body into the flames of a basement furnace. Wright portrayed Thomas not as a victim of racism, but as a result of it. *You made this violent monster*, Wright said to white America, *and now he is coming after you.*

It was a terrifying message, too harsh even for many black critics, yet the book was a bestseller, the first work by an African American to make the prestigious Book of the Month Club.

"Do you have any memories of the way he wrote and composed his novels?" Fabre asked Jane in his first letter. "[Is] there . . . any memory which you think might help me in the understanding of his personality?"[2]

Knowing Jane had been a Communist, Fabre worded his letter to her carefully about that sensitive point. "I have found out that American society is such that many fine people have had to, and still may have to, suffer because of their past opinions or political views," the Frenchman wrote. "You can be sure I shall treat any information of this kind as confidential."[3]

Jane thanked Fabre for the discretion. Her Communist past was not known in sunny, mainstream Santa Barbara. No one knew that she had lived in Russia for several months in the 1930s, or that she had been married to a paid Communist organizer.

Had all this been known, Jane may very well have lost her job as Santa Barbara city clerk, even in the early 1960s. Government workers across the country had been fired for their alleged Communist views and associations, and many were still required to sign loyalty oaths, swearing that they were "not now and have never been a member of the Communist Party." The Kennedy administration, long after the massive Red Scare of the 1950s, was still prosecuting alleged Communists for failing to register with the federal government.

"It is better to go silently about one's job and hope the

silent dogs will lie quietly and not bark in their sleep," Jane wrote Fabre.[4]

When Fabre's letter arrived, Jane was in her late fifties, her once-stunning beauty faded. Herbert was long dead, the victim of a stroke, possibly from countless police beatings in the head during his long career as a Communist agitator. Their marriage had produced five children, including a son aptly named Karl.

From Santa Barbara, Jane began to write Fabre long letters about Richard Wright, his life as a writer and a Communist Party member. She was really writing about an American revolution in the 1930s. Jane, Herbert, Wright, and many others were instruments in that struggle, which sought to end both racial discrimination and capitalism in America, all in one fell swoop.

Fabre was grateful for the information and would quote much of it in his biography of Wright. Her memories flowing, Jane kept writing, but Fabre eventually lost interest and dropped their correspondence. Jane still wanted to talk about the early 1930s, a "threadbare" but exhilarating time when men paced the streets in thin shoes and with empty stomachs, looking for work, their minds racing with the adrenaline of change in the blank slate that was the Great Depression.[5]

It was a decade of great writers such as Ernest Hemingway, Ezra Pound, and T. S. Eliot. The people were poor and hungry, but they seemed alive with art and literature and ideas. There was revolution in the air—real, radical possibilities.

This was the story Jane wanted someone to tell.

CHAPTER 1

The
FATHER

The story of Jane, her fame and her infamy, always seemed to center around her father, in the great contrast between them—the radical Communist and the American Legion commander.

It was almost as if John Emery's life had been scripted for a patriotic path. He was born on the Fourth of July in 1881 in the furniture-making city of Grand Rapids, Michigan. Patriotism was always the song he sang and the life he lived. It was more than just a belief for Emery. It was his persona, his occupation.

"I am for America, first, last and always," he would say.[1]

His father, John Emery Sr., was an immigrant from Scotland and the owner of a stable and long-lasting wallpaper and painting business in Grand Rapids.[2] It was a reputable entrepreneurial life, and his son followed that path but on a higher level, becoming a real-estate agent, developer, and insurance broker. John Emery Jr. was the kind of man who joined every civic group and every fraternal organization, and who ultimately was elected president of each group he joined. He was a natural leader.

Emery fathered two daughters, the younger named Esther. The family lived peacefully, respectfully, prosperously in Grand Rapids. Jane's chief memories of her childhood were idyllic: drifting asleep to the sound of her mother playing Schubert on the piano downstairs.[3]

Her father "loved to play with my sister and me," Jane recalled. "He romped with us, invented games which we played together." Her mother, Ethel, was "playfellow, teacher, comforter."[4] This upbringing made Jane's later conversion to Communism, her complete defiance of convention, all the more puzzling to so many. Why did she despise capitalism when it had given her such a comfortable, secure life?

Her father was of a generation that believed the United States was destined for greatness, destined to be a world leader, a country that could accomplish anything. And when the United States entered World War I in 1917, Emery was quick to sign up. This was the first time America would display its military prowess on the world stage, for all to see. Emery, quickly an officer, served in France with the Eighteenth Infantry's "Fighting First" Division. The American troops turned the tide of the war and forever established the United States as a world military power.[5]

But it was a strange, horrible war, and not only because of the poisonous gas, trenches, and absolute slaughter of troops on both sides. The war unleashed demons that would come back to haunt the United States, including Communism in Russia, fanatical nationalism in Germany, and fear and appeasement in Great Britain. These demons would lead to a second world war just two decades later. The war also fostered disenchantment among African Americans, who fought bravely, only to return to the same degree of racial prejudice they had left behind.

The Great War led to the formation of the American Legion, a group dedicated to supporting war veterans. The weary soldiers did not even wait until they were back on American soil to form the group, so urgently did they feel the need for an organization that would fight for veterans, make sure they were given proper help and respect, and see that their sacrifices would not be forgotten. The American Legion's first organizational meeting was held March 15 through 17, 1919, in Paris, just a few months after the armistice of November 11, 1918.[6] The organization's ranks would eventually exceed two million. Posts were established in virtually every city and town in the United States. But the American Legion would become, its critics later said, a jingoistic platform for blind patriotism. It would become an organization with a chip on its shoulder.

John Emery Jr. was among the casualties of the war, wounded in the left arm by a German shell in Argonne, France, on October 9, 1918, less than a month before the fighting ended. While he was lying on a stretcher waiting to be taken off the battlefield, the Germans fired a shell of mustard gas overhead, forcing Emery, then a major, to don his gas mask.[7]

Jane, his elder daughter, was only nine at the time. Years later, she would remember her mother's expression when she learned that her husband had been wounded. It wiped out the memories of parades, banners, and bugle calls when the war began.

John Emery returned home to Grand Rapids to a hero's welcome. But Jane was horrified by the sight of her "pale, thin, bandaged" father. She was "shaken with joy" to see him again. But he was not the same person, not the same father. And neither was Jane the same daughter.[8]

Jane was an extremely intelligent child who read voraciously. At the public library in Grand Rapids, she read "every book on the shelves. History and historical fiction fascinated me." But why was so much of history about war? she wondered. "Wars, wars, might making right," she remembered.[9] And here was her father, a symbol of war. It horrified Jane that her father, even wounded, vowed that he would fight again if his country needed him. He stated this flatly during speeches across Michigan. "We men are in the service for the rest of our lives," Emery said.

The young Jane believed her father should have taken an opposite approach. "I felt that he who had seen what war was should be the first to use all the influence at his command to avert any repetition of such horror," she later wrote.[10]

Yet John Emery's service in the war, his wounds, his hero status would be a boon to his career. He was elected to more boards, served with more organizations, including the Salvation Army. He won a seat on the Grand Rapids City Council. Naturally, he joined the American Legion. The Grand Rapids post was the second formed in the United States.

The American Legion fought for veterans. It fought for more hospitals for the wounded, for cash bonuses for those who served at low wages while others stayed home and worked in lucrative war-industry jobs. Robert Burns, a New York City accountant before the war, was one of those veterans who returned home to find no jobs. An ex-soldier "was looked upon as a sucker," Burns later wrote. "The wise guys stayed home, landed the good jobs or grew rich on war contracts."[11] Burns became a drifter and eventually a convict on the Georgia chain gang.

Burns was a white man. For black soldiers, the feeling of rejection, of betrayal after loyal, life-threatening military service in a foreign land, was even greater.

A young man from Chicago named Harry Haywood belonged to an all-black National Guard unit federalized during the war. On July 25, 1917, his unit was ordered to Camp Logan near Houston for training.[12]

The spirits of the black soldiers were dampened when they learned that a race riot was raging at Camp Logan involving black members of the Twenty-fourth Infantry Regiment. A black soldier had questioned a white police officer who was roughly arresting a black woman in Houston. White officers began beating the black soldier, a private.

"I beat that nigger until his heart got right," one of the white policemen later said. "He was a good nigger when I got through with him."[13]

A black military police officer, unarmed in deference to the white citizens of Houston, who feared black soldiers with guns, approached the white police officers, trying to intervene. The black officer was beaten and arrested as well.

The black soldiers at Camp Logan were outraged. Their white superiors, fearing revenge by the black troops, ordered the soldiers to surrender their arms, which they did. Black soldiers then killed a sergeant and retrieved their weapons before marching into town, searching for anyone who even looked like a policeman. They killed seventeen whites, thirteen of them policemen. Martial law was declared.

Subdued by a division of white soldiers with the help of armed white civilians, the black soldiers were taken to Fort Huachuca in Arizona. Thirteen were executed and forty-one sentenced to life in prison.

This was Harry Haywood's introduction to the United States Army as his regiment, the Eighth Illinois Infantry, headed to the same facility, Camp Logan, for training. The white community in Houston made it clear the black soldiers were not wanted. The chamber of commerce and scores of white citizens contacted the Texas congressional delegation and urged it to divert the black soldiers from Houston. Major General George Bell Jr. said it was Washington's decision but added, "I will say, however, that I do not believe any more Negro troops should be sent here."[14]

When the troop train crossed the Mason-Dixon line headed south to Houston, Haywood and his fellow black soldiers were still "brooding" over the Camp Logan riot. In Jonesboro, Arkansas, a crowd of white and black citizens greeted the troop train. "We were at our provocative best," Haywood remembered. "We threw kisses at white girls on the station platform."[15]

As the soldiers—required to leave their army-issued Springfield rifles on the train—walked to crowded stores near the station, some started looting. "In the stores, some bought, some stole," Haywood wrote. "This spontaneously evolved pattern was employed in raids on all stores in Jonesboro and at other stops along the road to Houston."

They arrived in Houston five days after the riot and were told their pay would be docked for the looted goods on the trip south.

Strangely, the racial atmosphere in Houston had cooled after the violence. Haywood attributed this to the black soldiers. "The whites, especially the police, had learned they couldn't treat all Black people as they had been used to treating local Blacks," he wrote.[16]

On the battlefront, Haywood and his fellow soldiers were attached to a French army unit that treated them as equals. The United States Army constantly warned the French to avoid fraternizing with the black soldiers, to keep them in their place. "Although a citizen of the United States, the black man is regarded by the white American as an inferior being," American general John J. Pershing wrote the French. "We must prevent the rise of any pronounced degree of intimacy between French officers and black officers. We must not eat with them, must not shake their hands or seek to talk or meet with them outside the requirements of military service."[17]

Despite these warnings from the Americans, Haywood liked the French and experienced little racism within their ranks. He served in the trenches, coping with constant struggle with lice and rats, but saw only light combat. He soon found himself discharged from the army and back at home, working as a waiter on the Michigan Central Railroad.

In ex-soldiers such as Robert Burns, Harry Haywood, and many others, the resentment would fester for years. As the Great Depression worsened in 1932, seventeen thousand veterans, called "the Bonus Army," camped in Washington to demand payment on the IOUs Congress had issued for their bonuses, which could not be redeemed until 1945. After a few violent clashes between the former servicemen and police, President Herbert Hoover ordered the army, led by

General Douglas MacArthur and six tanks, to drive the protesters and their families out of their camp. It was not until 1935 that the bonuses were paid.

The American Legion, its meeting halls cropping up across the country in small towns and larger cities, was a constant, powerful advocate for the ex-soldiers. Yet early on, the organization found itself involved in controversies that did not involve veterans. At times, the American Legion took on the air of a vigilante group.

In late 1919, a performance in John Emery's hometown of Grand Rapids by Fritz Kreisler, the Austrian violinist, was canceled after the American Legion objected to the appearance of an "enemy alien," even though the war had been over for more than a year.[18]

In January 1921, lawyers for the American Legion informed two Japanese families who purchased farms in Texas that they would have to leave. A Texas law, the attorneys said, prohibited "alien nonresidents" from owning farmland.[19]

Six months later, John Emery became national commander of the American Legion, succeeding F. W. Galbraith, who had been killed in an automobile accident. Emery was the third commander in the group's history. Now a national figure, he would lobby Congress to give veterans their cash bonuses, a debt the country owed the former soldiers for their sacrifice. He would dedicate war memorials across the United States. In a speech in Grand Rapids in June 1921, Emery vowed to fight the flow of immigrants to the United States "for the sake of our country's welfare."[20]

On Armistice Day, November 11, 1921, three years after the war had ended, Emery reminded the country to honor the veterans, particularly those who had died or were crippled in battle. "These are our heroes," Emery said, "our living monuments to America's ideals, to American principles, to American citizenship."

Emery wrote President Warren Harding a scathing letter in July 1921 warning against the pardoning of Eugene Debs, the Socialist labor leader who in 1918 had been convicted of espionage and sentenced to ten years in prison for making an antiwar speech, part of a sweeping crackdown on free speech during the war. While a prisoner at the Atlanta Federal Penitentiary, Debs had run for president in 1920 on the Socialist ticket and received nearly a million votes.[21] Releasing Debs would "do more to license a wholesale disregard of law and order than any one act the President might take," Emery wrote.

Late in 1922, despite the warning from the powerful American Legion, Harding, a Republican, commuted the sentences of Debs and twenty-three others prisoners who, according to a White House statement, had been jailed because they "opposed the war in one way or the other." Even the mainstream press called them political prisoners.

The job of American Legion commander was a high-profile position for Emery. He led some two hundred war veterans to France and Belgium in the summer of 1921, receiving a hero's welcome. In Brussels, King Albert bestowed upon Emery the Gold Medal of the Order of Leopold.[22]

But grumblings came from rank-and-file American Legion members that Emery and other top officers hogged the attention and perks on the trip. Emery, it was alleged, divided the touring group into a headquarters company for the high-ranking officers and four other companies for enlisted men, even though the war was long over and the men were no longer in the military. Emery even established a court-martial-like system to punish soldiers who were out of line on the trip. The headquarters company enjoyed the best of everything—accommodations, cars, medals—the enlisted men claimed. The men who had died in the war deserved the honors, not officers like Emery. Showing their symbolic displeasure on the voyage home, the enlisted men held "indignation meetings" and elected their own chairman of the expedition, snubbing Emery.[23]

In the fall, French general Ferdinand Foch, Allied supreme commander during the war, attended the American Legion's annual convention in Indianapolis and was greeted at the train station by an estimated fifty thousand Legionnaires.[24] As a follow-up to Emery's strongly worded letter to President Harding, the American Legion adopted a resolution opposing the release of Debs and other radicals. "If there is anyone here who dares to vote no, let him stand," Emery told the convention. No one stood. The Legionnaires called on state legislatures to require schoolteachers to take loyalty oaths. The Americanism Committee called for English to be the only language used in schools and for stronger regulation of "radical activities." It called for a law making it illegal to send anything in the mail that had an "un-American tendency."[25]

Barred from seeking a second term as commander, and unpopular anyway among the rank-and-file over the trip to France, Emery returned to Grand Rapids and soon entered politics. He ran for the United States Senate from Michigan, calling himself a "progressive Republican" and challenging incumbent Charles E. Townsend, whom Emery branded as a machine politician. Emery said his opponents offered him the job of Grand Rapids postmaster if he would drop out of the race, but he refused. Always, Emery appealed to veterans and promoted his own patriotism.

Emery lost the contest, coming in dead last. He returned to real estate in Grand Rapids.

Meanwhile, Jane was rapidly drifting away from her father's world view. In 1922, the year John Emery ran for the Senate, fourteen-year-old Jane won an essay contest. The topic was "What the U.S. Constitution Means to Me."[26] Jane concluded the essay with this sentence: "Rulership is in the hands of the people."

She stuck with that populist view, and as she grew older, it only deepened. She was not only horrified by war but began to notice economic disparities in the capitalist system her father epitomized, particularly as his development business flourished in the 1920s real-estate boom.

"Even in those early years," Jane would later write, "I observed what were to me at the time unaccountable inequalities among the children in my classes. Some were punch-faced, pale and shabbily dressed. Some had clothes better than mine. The shabby ones sometimes had difficulty getting the books they needed. They were sick and out of school often. All this I saw and in my child's mind wondered about the reasons for it."[27]

She began to disapprove of "a child's being given advantage not on his own merit but on the heels of his father's position in one economic category or another."

Jane attended community college in Grand Rapids before deciding in the fall of 1927 to transfer to the University of Michigan. She landed a part in a campus comedy called *On Approval*. Jane played Maria, a wealthy widow who auditions a potential husband for a month at her estate in Scotland. In the play, Jane wore red garters on both legs.

"She was tall and beautiful with black hair done into a chignon," Allan Seager, another Michigan student, later wrote in a fictional but largely accurate account of his brief relationship with Jane.[28]

In his story, Seager bets a fraternity brother all the beer he can drink that he can retrieve one of Jane's garters. Seager appears the next day at Jane's dressing-room door.

"She was in a black satin peignoir," Seager wrote, "her long hair over her shoulders, her face shining, ready for the makeup." He asks her for the garter, and she agrees, taking it off her leg and handing it to Seager. Her stocking immediately falls down. Seager suggests she pull the stocking up and tie a knot in it, which Jane does.

Seager later takes Jane to dinner, and they meet on campus to drink and kiss. Jane informs Seager that she is engaged to a fellow actor in the play, although she doesn't love the man.

Why, then, is she marrying him?

There are three reasons, says Jane: "One, it will get me away from my family. Two, I can lose my virginity in honor. Three, it will get me to New York."

In fact, Jane married Kenneth Sheldon White on New Year's Eve in 1927. They moved to New York to live with his parents. Jane wrote her parents, basically telling them good-bye forever.[29]

John Emery wrote back, "The air of finality in your letter sort of jolted a bit. Soldiers are taught to make a quick estimate of a situation and act accordingly. Your sad 'goodbye—I'm leaving you forever' attitude startles me. Why, honey?

I want always to be counted as one of your best friends. I want you to remember the latchstring of my dugout is always open to you and there will never be a time when what is mine isn't your's [*sic*] no matter how 'ornery' you get, no matter how much your modernist notions conflict with my old Victorian fundamentalist notions."

Jane's first marriage did not last long. Once Jane and Kenneth were out of the "golden haze" of the Michigan campus, both realized they were "hopelessly mismatched."[30]

In his short story, Seager finds Jane living with a married couple on East Fourth Street in New York. "I saw that she was dirty," Seager wrote. "Not a smudge here or there but the sheen of the unbathed."[31]

For money, Jane stakes out subway stations. "I would try to find prosperous-looking old gents and say, 'I'm terribly sorry. I seem to have left my purse at home. Would you . . . ?' "

She says she is writing a play and has not eaten at all that day, so Seager takes her out for an Italian meal. As they walk out the door of the apartment, he notices the book she is reading.

It is entitled, *The Decline of the West*.

CHAPTER 2

Music
from THE AIR

As Jane was striking out on her own during the late 1920s, defying her war-hero father, disowning her family, Herbert Newton was himself taking a radical path toward becoming a Communist revolutionary and the most improbable future son-in-law of John Emery, the former commander of the American Legion.

Newton was the grandson of American slaves. After the Civil War and freedom, his family migrated north from Virginia to Boston, where they created new lives, free from much of the racial oppression of the Deep South but still relegated to the bottom of the economic ladder. Herbert's father was a house painter and waiter, his mother a domestic servant, "both poverty stricken." Their four children "at various times helped out by making money at odd jobs," Newton recalled. Despite the poverty, the Newtons focused on education, ideas, music, possibilities. Newton was "brought up in the church," and although his mother eventually stopped attending, "she sent [her] children and continued to believe in God." Newton's father voted Republican but was not politically active.[1]

As early as age ten, Newton worked as an office boy. That job was followed by "too many to enumerate," including errand boy, berry picker, and newsboy.[2]

Newton's father died at age fifty-eight, when Herbert was fifteen years old. As the eldest male in his family, Herbert was forced to work full-time to support his mother and three younger siblings. He found jobs in a Boston wagon factory and, in the first of a lifetime of labor-management disputes, was fired for demanding paid holidays.[3] He then worked as a hotel elevator operator and bellhop.

Somehow, Newton found time to finish high school, attending night school and taking correspondence courses. He also learned how to play the piano, even to speak French. He was a Boy Scout.

In 1927, Newton finally landed a stable, coveted job with the United States Postal Service as a mailman. The post office then was a hotbed for African American Communists. Many of the leading black Communists in the United States, including Harry Haywood and the writer Richard Wright, worked there. These were all intelligent, restless men. Postal work, though it paid well, was considered by these men to be extremely tedious. They broke the monotony by discussing world events, racism, and Communism, which was no longer theory following the Russian Revolution in 1917.

Newton joined the Communist Party in Boston in 1926, when he was twenty-two years old. This was only nine years after the Communists gained control in Russia during World

War I, with help from Germany, which wanted Russia out of the war. The Germans helped the revolutionary Vladimir Lenin return to Russia in April 1917. Seven months later, Lenin led an uprising that seized control. Russia signed a peace treaty with Germany, prompting the United States to enter World War I. The United States and its allies won the war, but Communism was real now, in a huge country, and would haunt America for decades to come. Following the chaotic first few years after Lenin seized control, Communism stabilized in Russia in the 1920s under Joseph Stalin, although brutal suppression of opponents of the Communist system would continue to be a hallmark of his dictatorial regime.

Worldwide, this new Communism had an attraction. Quickly, two competing groups of former Socialists formed the Communist Party of the United States in 1919 in Chicago, a harbinger of the infighting that would plague the American movement throughout its history. The Communist International finally forced the two groups to merge in 1921, but split after split followed in the 1920s and 1930s until a solid front was created in 1940. Communists in the United States would always have trouble getting along.

The model for Communism was the *Communist Manifesto*, written by Karl Marx and Friedrich Engels in 1848 in response to the miserable lives of factory workers and miners in Europe. There was only one way to achieve happiness for the common man, Marx and Engels believed: give workers control of the government, and give government control of the factories and farms.

In 1920s Boston, this concept appealed to young Herbert Newton, who had known little but hard work and struggle, night and day, to pull out of the menial life of labor his parents had been saddled with. For African Americans in the United States, Communism had another appeal: it advocated complete racial equality. In Boston, Newton found that racial discrimination against blacks was not as severe as it was in the Deep South. Still, he encountered racism in the North, just as he would encounter it for the rest of his life. Segregation had in fact been codified into United States law with the 1896 Supreme Court decision in *Plessy v. Ferguson*, upholding "separate but equal" public facilities for whites and blacks. Segregation was also the law of the land in state statutes in the South, where African Americans lived under a system of apartheid that for most of them guaranteed a life of drudgery and poverty. If they resisted: lynching.

In much of the Deep South, it was difficult, if not impossible, for blacks to vote. Southern states, solidly Democratic, banned blacks from voting in the all-important Democratic primaries. Other laws went farther, seeking total disenfranchisement even in general elections. Blacks in the South were widely barred from serving on juries. Diseases such as malaria, pellagra, and syphilis were rampant. In both the North and the South, segregated neighborhoods reduced the supply of available housing for blacks, trapping them in substandard homes with no place to turn, a slumlord's dream.

In much of the South, even grueling textile-mill jobs were off-limits to blacks, reserved for the "Anglo-Saxon stock" of poor whites. African Americans faced large issues including lynching, housing, voting, a biased criminal justice system, and grossly inferior schools. But Southern blacks also encountered day-to-day hazards in matters as simple as walking down a sidewalk. Brushing against a white person, particularly a white woman, could be hazardous, and blacks had to be aware of this and develop strategies. Sometimes, the easiest thing to do was to avoid crowded sidewalks altogether and walk in the street. When going to the home of a white person, blacks were careful to knock on the back door, a gesture of subservience. When taken to and from work by their white employers, black domestic servants were required to sit in the backseat, a practice that lingered until the 1980s and possibly beyond. Blacks had to be careful to address white men as "Mister" but would provoke anger if they used the same courtesy title for a black man.

It was dangerous for blacks to be too successful financially or even to look too good, Benjamin Mays, a black man who later became president of Morehouse College, recalled from his childhood near Greenwood, South Carolina. One such person was a black Georgia farmer who split his money between two banks and refused to purchase a car so that whites would not be affronted by his affluence. When Mays was a junior in high school, he was standing outside a post office when a white doctor randomly struck him in the face, saying, "Get out of my way, you black rascal, you're trying to look too good anyway." Mays's crime was standing erect and wearing clean, although inexpensive, clothing. "A negro was not supposed to look neat and intelligent or to stand erect," Mays recalled.[4]

As Richard Wright would later describe in his novel *Native Son*, the rules of race affected the way blacks walked, talked, and thought, and even the direction of their eyes, which had to be pointed downward in the presence of a white person to show the proper respect. In Atlanta, department-store elevators were segregated, except for one store where, nonsensically, blacks were allowed to go up in the white elevator but not down, Mays recalled.

The rules encompassed physical and psychological edicts that for the simple purpose of survival were passed down from one generation of African Americans to the next.

"Why did I take it?" Mays asked himself after the white man struck him. "Why didn't I hit back? What would I have done if it had been another Negro who struck me?"[5]

As tempting as it was for Mays to retaliate, his mother had ingrained in him to stay out of trouble. At the same time, Mays realized that if he returned the blow, whites on that busy Saturday afternoon in Greenwood would have shot him dead, and the killer would never have been prosecuted.

Segregated trains and buses created no end of conflict. It is common knowledge today that blacks in the Deep South had to sit at the back of buses, but it was hardly that simple. The more important rule was that blacks could not sit in front of whites. Usually, only the very back row was reserved for blacks. If whites filled in some but not all the seats toward the back, blacks had to stand, even though there may have been empty seats throughout the bus. On trains, southbound passengers who purchased tickets in the North could sit wherever they chose until they crossed the Mason-Dixon line, at which point they were forced to move to a segregated rail car. It took a Supreme Court decision to stop railroads from placing black passengers behind curtains in the dining cars so that whites could not see them.

There was seemingly no end to the contradictory rules and customs, such as the requirement that black men take off their hats when approaching white women, while white men did not have to do so for black women. Courtesy titles

were an ongoing source of friction. As Urban League director in Tampa, Florida, Mays was criticized by whites for in-
troducing his own wife as "Mrs. Mays."

But no issue was more volatile, more deadly than sex between a black man and a white woman. Southern laws outlawed marriage between the races; it was not until 1967 that
these statutes were ruled unconstitutional by the Supreme
Court. Preserving white "racial purity" was the core tenet of
the Ku Klux Klan, which in 1922 kidnapped Alex Johnson, a
black bellhop in Dallas, Texas, who allegedly had sex with
a white woman. The Klansmen beat Johnson with a black-
snake whip, then used acid to burn *KKK* into his forehead.
He lived, fortunate that he was not outright lynched, as was
the case many times throughout the South. Sending a grim
message that was a symbol of their obsession with this issue,
lynchers sometimes castrated their black victims before killing them.

In many states, rape was punishable by death, a sentence
reserved exclusively for black men who raped white women,
and never applied to white men who raped black women.
At the same time, black families in the South were forced
to protect their wives and daughters from sexual advances
by white men, who were immune from any punishment, a
task made more difficult by the fact that black women often
worked in the homes of white families as domestic servants.

Benjamin Mays recalled that in his rural hometown in
South Carolina, "when one of my sisters went to the store,
one brother always went with her. As a rule, my father never
allowed my sisters to cook for white families."[6]

It was not a stretch of the imagination in the 1920s to

believe that long-oppressed African Americans would be attracted to Communism or any other ideology that might provide some hope of escaping the dehumanizing, long-lasting, and seemingly endless racism and poverty in the United States. None other than Lenin himself recognized this, writing that "the similarity of the economic position of the Negros with that of the former serfs in the agrarian centers of Russia is remarkable."[7] The fledgling American Communist Party, assisted directly by Moscow, saw early on that American blacks, particularly those in the South, were a prime target for recruitment.

In 1925, a year before Herbert Newton joined the party, forty black Communists met in Chicago under the banner of the American Negro Labor Congress. The group passed a resolution praising the Soviet Union. "The workers' government there is the first to bring into being full social, political and economic equality for all peoples," the resolution said.[8] The Communists recruited intelligent, well-spoken, educated blacks such as Herbert Newton. And the party did not offer just rhetoric and a membership card. It offered free education, world travel, a career.

Yet American labor unions warned blacks that the Communists were using them, misleading them to believe that "all their grievances will be remedied by overturning the government of the United States and installing a Soviet republic." Further, labor leaders said the Communists were instilling in blacks "the most pernicious doctrine—race hatred."[9]

A year after he joined the party, Newton left his job as a mailman and was on his way to the Soviet Union, chosen by the party for extensive training in Marxism at a school called the Communist University of the Toilers of the East, abbreviated as KUTV.[10]

It was not illegal to be a Communist in the United States, nor was it illegal for Americans to visit or study in the Soviet Union. Although America had withdrawn its diplomatic recognition of Russia after the 1917 revolution and would not restore it until 1933, numerous commercial exchanges still existed between the two countries in the 1920s. The Soviets recruited American contract workers to help upgrade their factories. One was a young black man named Robert Robinson, who in 1930 was working as a $140-per-month toolmaker for the Ford Motor Company in Detroit when the Soviets recruited him, raised his pay to $250 a month, and offered him free rent, a maid, and thirty days of annual vacation. It was an offer Robinson could not refuse.[11]

Although fewer than a hundred young American blacks accepted the Soviet Union's offer to study at KUTV, the very thought of it generated fearful headlines in the United States. These young men were to be trained as Communist revolutionaries and would be dispatched back to what seemed even to many whites as fertile ground among African Americans with a long list of grievances about their second-class status in the United States. Yet a white reader of the *Boston Herald* commented that "the constant wonder is that there are not more, considering the status of colored Americans." The way to discourage Communism among blacks, the letter writer said, was to "treat the Negro with more justice." If Americans wanted to fight Communism, the writer said, they should stop the lynchings, stop blacks from being burned alive at the stake, as was still happening in the South. This would be the way to save democracy. If the Communists indeed made inroads in the United States, it was the fault of America, not blacks, the writer said.[12]

Herbert Newton, young, self-educated, and handsome, left on his voyage to Russia in late 1927, all expenses paid by the Soviet Union. From the United States, he took a ship to Cherbourg, France. There, he boarded a train to Paris, then to Berlin, where he waited for his Soviet visa to arrive. He stayed in Berlin at the old, upscale Hotel Russischer Hof. Leo Tolstoy had been among the hotel's notable guests. "It's quite classy," Newton wrote his mother. "You have a boy posted at the revolving doors turning them around while you enter. In the dining room, the waiters do everything except eat your food."[13]

Newton liked the fact that Europeans were open with their class distinctions. "There isn't hypocrisy in Europe that there is in America," he wrote. "The Europeans make no attempt to hide their classes and they do not feign democracy."

He arrived in Moscow on the Monday afternoon after Thanksgiving and passed a physical and mental examination before checking in at the dormitory at KUTV.[14] The school was housed in central Moscow in the old Strastnoi Monastery, now known as Pushkin Square. There, students from all over the world gathered to be schooled as revolutionaries. The several famous KUTV graduates would include the Vietnamese nationalist Ho Chi Minh, who attended in 1923, and Chinese leader Deng Xiaoping, class of 1925.

Newton arrived at KUTV two years after the first African American students had enrolled. From 1925 to 1938, when KUTV was closed, the school counted fewer than a hundred black students.[15]

He spent the first few days as would a typical college student in a foreign land, "arranging our room, getting our meal tickets, learning the language."[16] Newton grew a beard. He learned to speak Russian and German and studied the theory of Marxism-Leninism. KUTV also offered classes in geography, mathematics, "historical materialism," and even light military training. The rigorous academics included as many as thirty hours of classes a week.

African Americans encountered racism in Russia, but it was different from that in the United States. It was not the law of the land, not so deeply embedded into the customs as in many areas of the United States. The Soviet government's strong official stance against racism meant that when it did arise, it could not be easily ignored.

Harry Haywood, the African American World War I veteran from Chicago, had arrived at KUTV in 1926, more than a year before Newton. Haywood was one of only eight African Americans in Moscow at the time. The group included Haywood's brother Otto Hall, a former steel worker from Ohio named Jim Farmer, and a woman from the state of Georgia named Emma Harris. Before the revolution, Harris had toured Moscow with a vaudeville act and stayed behind when her manager abandoned the dance troupe. She subsequently became the madam of a brothel for noblemen. After the revolution, Harris became a textile worker. She longed to return to America. Once a month, the African American KUTV students pooled their money so that Harris could provide them a home-cooked meal.

Blacks were so rare in Moscow that they attracted crowds of curious, friendly onlookers if they so much as stopped on the street to greet a friend.

Only once in his more than three years living in Russia did Haywood encounter racism. On a streetcar, a drunken man muttered, "Black devils in our country." Other passengers, outraged by the comment, ordered the conductor to stop the streetcar. "How dare you, you scum, insult people who are the guests of our country," one of them said to the drunk.[17] The passengers held an impromptu meeting and decided to drop the drunk off at the next police station. By then, he had sobered up and was apologizing. Haywood decided not to press charges. "We'll keep him overnight," the police officer told Haywood. "Perhaps this will be a lesson to him."

Whites beat Robert Robinson, the former Ford factory worker recruited by the Russians. The attackers threatened to drown Robinson in the Volga River. But these were fellow American contract workers, not Russians. A Stalingrad newspaper denounced the attacks and the "social poison" of American racism. Workers staged a protest rally and spoke on the evils of racism.[18]

In the Soviet Union, African Americans could freely date and even marry white women, which in states such as Virginia, Mississippi, Alabama, and Georgia was illegal and could have led to their lynching.

In a huge contrast to their lives in the United States, where blacks were at best tolerated by society and at worst persecuted, the African American KUTV students often found themselves treated as heroes, even celebrities, by the Russians.

"I got a wonderful reception everywhere I went," Newton wrote his mother during a summer tour of the Soviet Union. "One day I was invited to supper by a collective of university students living a communal life. The next day the Young Pioneers and Young Communists marched with a Red Army band to my hotel to greet me. Another day, I was given a front seat at a concert of an inventor who takes music from the air."[19]

Newton saw a Soviet Union brimming with optimism, a nation that was building entire cities around massive factories for farm equipment and other machinery. The redistribution of wealth under Communism modernized and mechanized the Soviet Union in a massive economic transformation.

"Three things I will never forget," Newton wrote. "One was a Pioneer, a girl not more than 12 years old, giving a report on the anniversary of the Paris commune. She spoke about the industrialization of the country, development of agriculture, the necessity of raising the cultural level of the masses, the international situation."[20]

Newton traveled with a translator while he was learning Russian. Once, the translator was sick and Newton surprised himself by giving a speech in Russian.

When he returned to Moscow after touring the country, Newton retained a dizzying image of a Soviet Union that was bursting with energy ten years after the revolution. "Even now my head sometimes reminisces of laughing Pioneers, youthful students, curious workers, applauding audiences, flying factory wheels," he wrote.

The KUTV students celebrated Halloween, even Christmas, although religion had no real place in the Soviet Union. "The government, it is true, has no need of churches or holidays and as a result church attendance has dwindled remarkably," Newton wrote. "Nevertheless, the old ideology of a superstitious age still hangs over."

Newton wrote home frequently asking for books, poetry in particular. He wanted to learn how to cook so he could make Boston baked beans for his comrades. He told his mother not to worry about his health, since hospitals, doctors, and even dandruff shampoo were provided for free in the Soviet Union. He kept up with news in the United States by reading the *New York Times*. His widowed mother wrote Herbert asking for money, but he replied that all he had were Russian rubles, worthless in the United States.

Not surprisingly, the United States Postal Service fired Newton while he was in Russia. Newton sent a family member to retrieve his postal uniform from a coworker's locker.

By American standards, life in the Soviet Union was shabby for the KUTV students. They complained of bedbugs, a lack of vegetables, a shortage of mild hand soap, and the bitter cold. They also requested new courses on "American Imperialism" in their curriculum.[21]

After six months at KUTV, Newton graduated to the much more prestigious Lenin School, where he was scheduled for advanced studies over the next thirty months before returning to the United States.

The Soviet Union's interest in African Americans intensified with a bold, ambitious plan: a separate black nation in the American South. The Russians needed an African American face for this idea, and Harry Haywood, Newton's fellow student at the Lenin School, was given the honor.

"Blacks were essentially an oppressed nation," the Soviets drilled into Haywood. "Therefore it was the duty of the party to channel the movement in a revolutionary direction by raising and supporting the slogan of the right of self determination." The simple fact was that many regions of the American South had more blacks than whites. Blacks were disenfranchised and often could not walk down a sidewalk, find a seat on a bus or train, or take an elevator without facing a confrontation with a white person.[22]

While the Soviets were "anxious to recruit at least one Black to support their position," Haywood was unsure about the concept, believing it was "far-fetched and not consonant with American reality." Haywood's brother, Otto Hall, also disagreed with the idea of a black nation. Blacks, Otto said, were not a suppressed nation but rather a suppressed race that wanted not independence from the United States but equal rights within it.[23] Also opposing the idea was Lovett Fort-Whiteman, a black Texan and early Communist who had served as an American recruiter for KUTV. He put forward perhaps the more practical idea of recruiting Southern blacks to Communism after they migrated to Northern cities, rather than in the brutal atmosphere of Dixie.

The Communists argued Haywood down. He soon supported the right of Southern blacks to determine for themselves whether or not to become a separate nation. Marcus Garvey's back-to-Africa movement was dead, but it had reflected true black nationalism in the United States, Haywood argued. He was the first American Communist to endorse that policy. It made him a party star, while critics such as Otto Hall and Lovett Fort-Whiteman were warned that they must work to implement the plan, even though they did not agree with it.

In the summer of 1928, the Sixth Congress of the Communist International, meeting in Moscow, endorsed the right of self-determination for American blacks. Herbert Newton was there. He was impressed by delegates from all over the world, of different races, speaking different languages, all committed to the common goal of Communism. "The organization of Negro masses to fight against oppression is most likely to be affected," Newton wrote his mother in Boston after the Sixth Congress.[24]

The fight for a new black nation was under way. It would be up to young Moscow-trained revolutionaries such as Newton and Haywood to implement the plan when they returned to the United States. World Communism was the ultimate goal of the Soviet Union, but if regions of the United States could be picked off piece by piece, all the better, as that would provide a North American foothold for the larger movement. Yet Haywood's initial reticence and the outright opposition by other African American Communists who knew their race and their country were possible signs that the Soviets did not really understand their target audience. Perhaps blacks in the South were not the same as Russian serfs after all.

Newton returned to the United States in 1929 without completing his studies at the Lenin School. The record is unclear on why he left before his scheduled graduation in June 1930.

Records in the Russian archives do reveal that Newton was married while in the Soviet Union, to a woman named Nechama. A controversy arose in early 1929 when Nechama was found living in the room of a fellow student identified as "Comrade Talmant." Talmant was reprimanded by the party, accused of trying to have his room automatically transferred to Nechama after he graduated in two years. At Newton's behest, B. D. Wolfe, American representative to the Executive

Committee of the Communist International, wrote a letter to the Central Control Commission of the Communist Party of the Soviet Union defending Talmant. Nechama was planning on going to the United States to be with Newton in June 1930, Wolfe wrote. Perhaps Nechama had different ideas. At any rate, the marriage did not last. Newton and Nechama were divorced for "alienated affections."[25]

Newton would later write that he left the Lenin School early to help unite the Communist Party of the United States, which was experiencing another of its frequent factional fights. For such an important mission, the party did not manage to immediately find a paid position for Newton after he arrived home. Although he worked full-time as a party functionary, he was also "selling household goods from house to house to make ends meet." It was not until 1930 that Newton landed a paid position in New York as associate editor of *The Liberator*, the official organ of the party's American Negro Labor Congress, with offices at 799 Broadway. The American Negro Labor Congress was founded by Lovett Fort-Whiteman, the black Texan, "to gather, to mobilize, and to coordinate into a fighting machine the most enlightened and militant and class-conscious workers of the race." [26]

Upon the collapse of the stock market in the fall of 1929 and the subsequent Great Depression, the United States was now far different from when Newton had left for Moscow in 1927.

When Harry Haywood returned from the Soviet Union in late 1930, he now spoke English with a Russian accent, after nearly four years away. He could not believe how shabby the United States appeared, the unemployed living in collections of makeshift shacks called "Hoovervilles," sad faces everywhere. "Despair seemed written on their faces," Haywood said. With capitalism seemingly on the ropes, the iron was hot for Communism.[27]

Newton was not back in the United States long before he asked to return to Moscow to finish his studies at the Lenin School, saying that the mission of uniting the American party had been accomplished. "Factionalism is liquidated in our party and we are now consolidating our forces for the present struggles and the greater ones to come," Newton wrote on May 14, 1930, to Lenin School director Klavdiia Kirsanova. "The whole Party is being mobilized to lead the American workers into militant struggle."[28]

The party, however, had a different mission in mind for Newton. He would be sent to the American South.

It was time to start a revolution.

CHAPTER 3

The
Atlanta SIX

Soon after Herbert Newton crossed the Mason-Dixon line on his trip south, he experienced the harsh reality of Jim Crow, Dixie's system of racial segregation. In Richmond, Virginia, in the state where Newton's grandparents had been slaves, he was promptly ordered to sit at the back of a bus and was kicked out of a theater and a public library.

"I wondered how the Southern Negroes take it," Newton wrote his mother back in Boston.[1] "I asked one and his opinion seems to be the opinion of the majority. They look upon Jim Crowism as something that [is] divined of God, that is natural and has to be. They don't suffer from Jim Crowism. They take it as a matter of course."

Many whites, self-servingly, would have agreed with Newton that Southern blacks were a hardy, happy people who didn't mind segregation. "Possessed of a cheerful philosophy unmatched by any other racial group, the negro, free today to live where he will, lingers contentedly in Georgia," a 1936 Georgia guidebook said, illustrating the item with a picture of blacks on a possum hunt.[2]

Yet many others disagreed. Jim Crow was a maddening form of psychological and physical torture, Richard Wright and Benjamin Mays, who both lived under the system, would later write. Yet Wright, Mays, and Newton all asked the same fundamental question: how did they take it?

Amid these larger long-term issues, Newton spotted immediate opportunity for Communist Party recruitment, for the revolution. Yes, Southern blacks lived under Jim Crow, seemingly without resistance, seemingly accepting the system. But beneath the surface, blacks held a "deep resentment" of the white man, which "properly directed could be used to completely destroy the whole system of Jim Crowism," Newton wrote his mother.[3]

He saw his job as taking that resentment and "directing it in proper channels." The Great Depression only made his task easier. "In the South, conditions were always bad for the Negroes," Newton wrote. "Now they are worse and still growing worse. The Negroes feel that something must be done and they welcome organization. They idolize anyone who helps improve their condition. An old man said to me, 'God bless you, my son.' "[4]

Newton was now gaining practical experience as an in-the-field revolutionary. Combined with his theoretical knowledge from studying in Moscow, this would allow him to lead the fight against "race prejudice, wage slavery and unemployment."

He arrived in Atlanta in May, using his revolutionary name, Gilmer Brady. Atlanta was then a provincial railroad city of about three hundred thousand people, a third of them black. It was the home of both Coca-Cola and the national Ku Klux Klan.

Newton joined a small group of Communists who were passing out leaflets and holding recruitment meetings. They made speeches against the lynching of blacks and spoke in favor of textile unions.

One tactical disadvantage for these young Communists was that they were largely barred from black churches, the center of the African American community's political and social life, then and now. It was no secret that Communism discouraged religion of any kind. Communists either did not understand the depth of spiritualism among blacks in the South or chose to ignore it. Many Southern blacks would always look upon Communists with suspicion, even if they agreed with the larger overall goal of racial equality.

Benjamin Mays was one of those who despised Jim Crow but at the same time had no use for Communism. Mays, the son of a South Carolina sharecropper, went on to become an ordained Baptist minister with a doctorate in theology from the University of Chicago. Before accepting the presidency of Morehouse College, he was dean of the Howard University School of Religion. His mother, a former slave who could not read or write, led the children in prayer each night. As a teenager plowing under the moonlight, Mays sometimes stopped and prayed that God would find a way for him to receive an education.[5] He understood that, after the horrors of slavery, some blacks, including his wife's grandfather, did not believe there was a God. But Mays countered that it was "the justice of God" that freed the slaves.[6]

Newton and his Communist colleagues who ventured

south were not religious, but what they did have was courage. This was hostile country. If Southern blacks were largely indifferent to Communists, many white residents of Atlanta viewed them as devils incarnate, threatening everything the South held sacred: religion, racial segregation, and capitalism. The county prosecutor in Atlanta , John Boykin, was a former member of the Ku Klux Klan who stated that it was just another civic club. Many politicians and law-enforcement officers were also current or former Klan members. While Communists in the North were largely tolerated by the white establishment, no such tolerance existed in the South. Communists were to be stamped out by any means necessary.

Earlier in the spring of 1930, two white Communists, Joe Carr and M. H. Powers, had been arrested in Atlanta and charged with attempting to incite insurrection under a Reconstruction-era law designed to control newly freed slaves. Powers, of Saint Paul, Minnesota, was twenty-three, a married father of two. Carr was nineteen and had worked in the West Virginia coal mines from the age of eleven.[7]

As the Great Depression worsened, the two men were distributing leaflets announcing a mass meeting on the party's demand for relief payments to the unemployed. In Georgia, that was a capital offense. If convicted, the young Communists faced death in the electric chair. In Georgia at the time, executions were routinely carried out within six weeks of arrest, barring appeals.

Another white Communist, Mary Licht, organized a meeting to protest the arrests of Carr and Powers. Licht, then twenty, was using the revolutionary name of Mary Dalton. She, like many young Communists at the time, was a graduate of the school of hard knocks. At age fourteen, she had been forced to take an office job to support her widowed mother and younger siblings. Attracted to the Communist cause, she had traveled south to recruit members to the National Textile Workers Union.[8] In Atlanta, the target was the Fulton Bag and Cotton Mills, located in a community called Cabbagetown, east of downtown. The plant was operating at part-time capacity as the Great Depression sapped business.

Newton was scheduled to speak at the meeting protesting the arrests of Carr and Powers, as was Anne Burlak, a party organizer in South Carolina whose nickname was "the Red Flame," both for the color of her hair and her fiery speeches.

Burlak, the daughter of Ukrainian immigrants, was born in Pennsylvania coal country and retained vivid memories of her family's hardships. Her father worked twelve hours a day for low wages in the dangerous mines, the family living in a run-down wooden company-owned house.[9]

In 1925, Burlak quit school at age fourteen to work in a textile mill not only to help her family make ends meet but to save money for college. Her pay for a fifty-four-hour workweek was nine dollars. Men earned twelve dollars weekly for the same job.

The noise of a hundred looms running at the same time meant that "one can only speak by shouting right into the ear of another person." After a full day of work, Burlak would leave the factory temporarily deaf. The factory conditions and wage issues prompted her to become a union organizer and a Communist at an early age, a typical story.[10]

The fourth person scheduled to speak at the Atlanta meeting was Henry Storey, a thirty-four-year-old black Communist from Washington County, Georgia, who had started picking cotton at age six and had only four years of education. Storey, like Harry Haywood, was among the black men radicalized by their experiences as soldiers in World War I. Storey was drafted into the army and served twenty-three months in France before returning to jobs in lumber mills in Georgia and steel mills in Ohio. He joined the party in 1929 and was working in an Atlanta print shop at the time of the Atlanta rally.[11]

With two black men—Newton and Storey—and two white women—Burlak and Licht—scheduled to speak, the Communists were clearly asking for trouble in Atlanta. On May 21, the four gathered at a meeting room on Auburn Avenue, a black business and residential area where a future civil rights leader named Martin Luther King Jr. was born on January 15, 1929.

Nearly a hundred people filled the meeting hall. The four Communists, sitting together on a platform, did not observe local custom. "Black and white workers sat wherever they wished," Burlak recalled.[12] A local white couple, Julius and Lizette Klarin, sold copies of the Communist newspapers *Daily Worker* and *The Liberator*.

As Storey opened the meeting, Atlanta police led by Captain Grover Fain "burst into the hall and placed the four of us on the platform under arrest," Burlak remembered.[13] Fain would later be fired from the force for "use of intoxicants." When he died in 1940, he left his life insurance and police pension to a woman other than his wife, with whom he had been "boarding" for the previous twelve years. Fain left his wife the princely sum of one dollar.[14]

When the officers placed Newton and Storey in a separate

police car, Licht and Burlak protested, fearing the two black men would be lynched. But they were all taken to the local jail, a "medieval looking stone structure with a tower."[15]

Newton, Storey, Licht, and Burlak were charged with attempting insurrection. They, too, faced the death penalty. Along with Powers and Carr, the group was called "the Atlanta Six." Within Communists ranks, Newton and his fellow defendants were now celebrities. Yes, the Atlanta Six faced the possibility of death in the Georgia electric chair, but their arrests marked a huge public-relations coup for the Communists, exposing internationally what appeared to be the great hypocrisy of the American creed. Six people facing a death penalty for holding a meeting, for passing out leaflets? That did not have the appearance of the "free country" the United States so proudly claimed to be.

At the jail, the prisoners were segregated by race and gender. In the women's dormitory, Burlak and Licht spent the night listening to a fellow inmate "arguing with some imaginary person, laughing hysterically." The woman was insane, the victim of an advanced case of syphilis.[16]

At a hearing the next day, a judge denied bond for the Communists.

"We were held incommunicado—no visitors, no mail, no newspapers," Burlak remembered. She blamed the harsh prosecution on the mill owners, who feared the union and were determined to preserve "starvation wages and miserable work conditions."[17]

A Communist-affiliated group, International Labor Defense, hired lawyers. The American Civil Liberties Union also joined the fight.

It was not until June 17, nearly a month after his arrest,

that Newton was able to write a letter to his family in Boston. "Trouble? Who said anything about trouble?" he joked. "Talk about free hotels, this is one of the state's finest."[18]

On a more serious note, however, he added, "You have no idea how much work there is to be done and especially down this way and how few forces there are to do it with."

Isolated from the news, Burlak and Licht requested copies of the *New York Times*, but the jailer was horrified. "That radical newspaper? Not on your life." Even the *Atlanta Constitution* was banned, leaving the women with only magazines such as *True Confessions*. They played solitaire for hours.

The indictment portrayed the Atlanta Six as far more than textile-union organizers, quoting the literature the Communists were distributing in Atlanta, which called for "full political, social and racial equality for the Negro workers." The pamphlets urged citizens to "smash the National Guard" and "defend the Soviet Union," according to the indictment.[19] The Communists were, the indictment flatly stated, trying to incite insurrection "for the establishment of the Soviet Union and the Communist Soviet Government in place thereof."

As reactionary and racist as the Georgia prosecutors were, they were largely correct about the motives of the Atlanta Six. They had no idea who Newton was, or even that his name was in fact Newton, or that he had recently returned from more than two years of training in the Soviet Union.

Violent overthrow of the government may have been the ultimate goal. But the Atlanta Six hadn't killed or injured anyone. All they did was pass out pamphlets and hold meetings. Where was the line between free speech and attempted insurrection? That was the larger legal question that would be resolved in the American courts.

It was almost six weeks before lawyers arranged bail for the Atlanta Six. Newton wasted no time in leaving Dixie for New York City, where he wrote his mother on July 1 from the safe confines of the American Negro Labor Congress at 799 Broadway. "Well my vacation is ended and I am back to work," he wrote. "I am told that with the exception of being a little thinner, I look all right. I am glad to be away from the Jim Crow South."[20]

Although the Atlanta Six faced possible death sentences, their arrests marked a victory for the Communists, a classic case of "agitprop"—a combination of agitation and propaganda. Throughout his career, Newton would describe himself either as an "agitprop director" or a "revolutionary journalist," the two jobs going hand in hand.

The Atlanta campaign had indeed agitated local authorities, stirring their emotions and prompting them to arrest and indict the Atlanta Six on capital charges, all for holding a meeting and passing out brochures. Anne Burlak, the first of the group to be released on bail, was asked to speak at the June 1930 convention of the American Communist Party. She received a standing ovation.

Newton used *The Liberator* to capitalize on the arrests. "The bosses are trying to send six Negro and white organizers to the electric chair all for the 'crime' of organizing workers in the South," Newton wrote shortly after he was released. "But no number of lynchings will keep us from carrying on our work."[21]

The American Communists did not ask this question: what would Stalin have done if the situation were reversed?

Would he have allowed capitalist organizers free rein in Russia? The answer would become clear later in the 1930s, when Stalin killed and imprisoned millions of his country's citizens—"spies, murderers and wreckers"—whom he believed were agents of capitalist opponents of Communism.

The United States, however, was supposed to operate on a higher plane than the Soviet dictator. Even some mainstream white citizens and media in the South believed the Atlanta prosecutors were going too far. The *Memphis Commercial Appeal* said the Atlanta Six case did "violence to the Constitution and to the spirit of Liberty." In Atlanta, a group of sixty-two ministers, college professors, and other prominent citizens signed a statement condemning the arrests. "The undersigned do not support the revolutionary philosophy and tactics of the Communist Party," the statement emphasized. "Yet we believe the communists should be protected in their constitutional rights of free speech and assemblage."[22]

Normally, Georgia prosecutors moved quickly in death-penalty cases. But surprisingly, they did not rush to bring the Atlanta Six to trial.

In her unpublished memoirs, Burlak speculated that Georgia officials did not like the optics of this case: two black men, two white women, two white men.[23]

Perhaps that was too much perceived unity for prosecutors to stomach.

CHAPTER 4

The Greatest
HAPPINESS

With a death penalty charge still hanging over his head and no way of knowing when or if Georgia prosecutors might call the case to trial, Herbert Newton returned to the world of Communist agitation and propaganda.

He was now a Communist folk hero, as evidenced by a rally of 2,500 people in New York's Union Square just a few weeks after Newton was released on bail from the Atlanta jail. Under the watchful eyes of New York City police commissioner Edward Mulrooney and 130 police officers bearing night sticks, Newton spoke at a rally as protesters displayed a mock electric chair with a sign that read, "The Atlanta Six Must Not Die."[1]

That November, Newton attended the party's American Negro Labor Congress in St. Louis, as did fellow Atlanta Sixer Mary Licht, a.k.a. Mary Dalton, and Harry Haywood, Newton's school colleague from Moscow. The official topic of the conference was lynching, but Haywood introduced a resolution, read aloud by Licht, calling for self-determination for blacks in the South. They were, the resolution said, "an oppressed nation struggling against U.S. Imperialism." The statement called for "confiscation of the land" to help small farmers, black and white, and for "death to the lynchers." The crowd cheered.[2]

Newton was among five hundred Communists who demonstrated on Capitol Hill in Washington on December 2, 1930, demanding an end to all restrictions on immigration. He presented a petition to Speaker of the House Nicholas Longworth. At one point, police fired tear gas to disperse the crowd.[3]

This would be Herbert Newton's world for the rest of his life: demonstrations, petitions, tear gas, and night sticks, sometimes accompanied by blows to the head.

While Newton was in Russia, in an Atlanta jail cell, and then back on the streets, Jane was struggling through two short-lived marriages.

She dropped out of the University of Michigan in late 1927, just about the same time Herbert was headed for Moscow. On New Year's Eve, a few weeks after Herbert arrived at the Communist University of the Toilers of the East to begin his revolutionary training, Jane married Kenneth Sheldon White, a fellow Michigan student who had performed with her in the university rendition of Frederick Lonsdale's play, *On Approval*. White played the suitor to Jane's ill-tempered English lady, Maria.

Jane had been restless in college and was ready for self-education. "I felt that I needed some time for thoughtful co-ordination of my academic education which I was constantly acquiring by independent reading," she would recall.[4] She also wanted to live in New York, to be independent from her parents, particularly her domineering father, and to "lose my virginity in honor."[5]

Jane and Kenneth were married in Grand Rapids by the minister in the church she had joined at age twelve. The newlyweds moved in with Kenneth's parents in New York. It did not take long for Jane to realize this was a mistake, as the "golden haze" of a college romance quickly faded. "We soon found ourselves not the congenial happy couple we thought ourselves to be but a hopelessly mismatched pair caught in a marriage in which neither of us could be happy," she wrote. The marriage, she later confessed, was a "sad mistake. It caused both of us pain and was a source of grief for our parents as well."[6]

After the marriage ended, Jane made her way to Chicago, where she met a white musician named William W. Lysacht, "a sensitive, high-spirited and very intelligent person."[7] Jane was a writer focusing on poetry at the time, and Lysacht was a pianist. They married and were happy for a while, but this union, like the first, would be short.

"We made the error of mistaking friendship, sound and affectionate as it was, for a love-justifying marriage," Jane wrote. "When we departed, there was no rancor between us, only disappointment for me and I believe for him as well." At the age of twenty-six, Jane found herself twice divorced and at a crossroads in her life.

It was in Chicago that Jane became a Communist. In the fall of 1931, as the world economy collapsed, Jane and a small circle of friends, some of them students, looked for respite from the grim reality of the Great Depression and fantasized about living on a desert island. One member of the group, a Russian who had fought in the revolution, offered that this paradise already existed. It was the Soviet Union.

"There, a plain man has a chance to work and live without worrying about old age, illness and unemployment," the Russian said. "All those dangers are done away there."

Jane studied the fathers of Communism, Karl Marx and Friedrich Engels. She concluded that the Communist Party was "the most reliable organization for attaining the greatest happiness for the greatest number of people." She began working with International Labor Defense, the legal arm of the party defending Newton and the other members of the Atlanta Six.

Meanwhile, the American South was erupting again in a case that would arguably mark the peak of the Communist Party's efforts there. It would put the party and International Labor Defense in the world spotlight.

On March 25, 1931, two white unemployed mill workers from Huntsville, Alabama, Ruby Bates and Victoria Price, hopped a freight train home from Chattanooga, Tennessee, where they had traveled to look for work. They were in a boxcar with several white men when a group of black men allegedly swarmed in, threw the white men off the train, and proceeded to rape the two white women. The white men contacted police, who stopped the train in the town of Scottsboro, Alabama, and arrested nine black passengers, ranging in age from thirteen to twenty-five. Less than two weeks after their arrest, eight of the nine were tried, convicted, and sentenced to death. No blacks were on the jury. In fact, "the oldest citizens of Scottsboro said they could not recall a time when a negro sat on a jury." In a county of thirty-six thousand people, there were only twenty-five black voters.[8]

As the Scottsboro trial was about to begin for the eight defendants six days after they were indicted, it wasn't even clear if the men had lawyers. When the judge asked if both sides were ready, no one answered for the defense. Finally, a local lawyer stepped forward and said, "I will go ahead and help do anything I can do." The United States Supreme Court, citing the "casual fashion" in which men facing the death penalty were provided attorneys, would later order new trials.[9]

The NAACP, the nation's premier civil rights organization, and one that specialized in fighting discrimination through the courts, was slow to react, even though it was hard to imagine a more egregious case.

But the Communists pounced. William Patterson, a lawyer by trade who had been a classmate of Newton's in Russia and was now executive secretary of International Labor Defense, convinced one of the top criminal lawyers in the nation, Samuel Leibowitz of New York, to represent the defendants at no fee. Leibowitz made clear, however, that he was not endorsing Communism but was taking the case because it centered on "the basic rights of man."[10]

Early intervention by the Communists saved the Scottsboro defendants from the electric chair. None was ever executed, although several served lengthy prison sentences. The Communists credited mass protests throughout the world with preventing the executions. They often ridiculed the American court system as a pawn of the ruling class. But it was actually both—the protests and the American legal system—that prevented the Scottsboro men from dying in the electric chair. Despite the racism of the Deep

South, the defendants still had the protection of the Constitution and the federal court system designed to defend it. That system did not always work, and when it worked, it often moved slowly. But as Scottsboro proved, it could be an effective tool of justice.

Still, Scottsboro was a propaganda bonanza for the Communists, who would proudly parade the mother of two of the Scottsboro defendants through the streets of Moscow.

As the party's momentum and profile in the United States increased, Newton was transferred in early 1932 to Chicago. Still corresponding directly with the Russians, still using the revolutionary name Gilmer Brady, he updated his résumé with the title of "agitprop director."

Chicago was then a city of about 3.3 million people. The once-booming metropolis would remain stagnant throughout the entire decade of the 1930s, so deep were the effects of the Great Depression. It would remain a magnet for blacks—including would-be writer Richard Wright—who were fleeing the oppressive South.

In debating the wisdom of pushing for a separate black nation in the American South, the young black Communist Lovett Fort-Whiteman had proposed the perhaps more practical idea of recruiting Southern blacks once they arrived in the North. Chicago would be the place to do that, and Newton was now there.

As the economy continued to deteriorate, the Chicago press wrote of charities going broke, of "the city and county throwing thousands of people out of homes," and of police who were reluctant to arrest "citizens begging not to be allowed to starve."[11] The policemen themselves had not been paid and were "on the verge of starvation," a press account said.

If ever there was proof that capitalism had collapsed, this was it. If ever there was a good time for the Communists to recruit new members, this was it.

In early January, Newton led a demonstration of two hundred desperate people outside the offices of the Illinois Emergency Relief Commission. The protesters demanded unemployment benefits of at least $15 a week and $150 in cash to make it through the winter, as well as an end to racial discrimination in relief programs. Three policemen were injured in the protest, and "a number of citizens were beaten and bruised."[12]

Amid these desperate times, Jane met Herbert.

Jane was in a bookstore when the "extremely handsome" Newton walked in. "He reminded me of paintings by a young Mexican artist, Francis Angela," Jane said.[13]

There was a widespread belief, a fear, among white people at the time that the Communists were using attractive white women to lure black men into the party. As a graduate student at the University of Chicago, Benjamin Mays, who never supported the Communist movement, remarked on "the ease with which communist girls socialized with black men." Yet Mays was never tempted by the white Communist women.[14]

Clearly, Jane had not been dispatched by the party to recruit Newton, who was already as devout a Communist as one could be, a paid career man. Jane would later point out that while the Communist Party supported equal rights for blacks, it did not view interracial marriage as a means to that end. "Intermarriage will not solve the problem of the oppression of this great people," she would write.[15]

Jane and Herbert became good friends and attended forums and lectures in Chicago. Newton told Jane about his time in the Soviet Union and the "absence of discrimination against men because of their race or nationality."[16]

Newton was a serious man, Jane remembered, who did not smoke or drink and who "cares little for parties or light entertainment. Best of all, he likes to read and play chess in his leisure."

Theirs would always be an intellectual, erudite relationship based on books, ideas, and thoughts of the United States after the revolution, which they believed would break out in time.

Their courtship began in 1932, a pivotal year for the Communist Party and for the nation at large. With a national election coming up in the fall, there was social unrest throughout the United States as the Great Depression worsened. Without jobs, sometimes without homes or food, men and women who might normally never think of revolution were in the position of having few other options. And thanks to high-profile cases such as Scottsboro and the Atlanta Six, the Communists were succeeding in illuminating the hypocrisy of the United States, supposedly the land of the free.

Despite the potential death sentences hanging over the heads of Newton and the five other defendants in the Atlanta Six, the Communists kept goading the South. The South was indeed fertile ground, now more than ever.

CHAPTER 5

P.O. Box 339

As low as the economy had slumped in Chicago and in the North in general, it was even worse in the Deep South. The Great Depression threatened to destabilize Southern society.

This was the summer of 1932, during the brutal period between the stock-market crash in October 1929 and the beginning of the New Deal's massive relief programs and creation of a vast social safety net, which would begin in 1933. A national election was on the way that fall, with President Hoover clearly on his way out and Franklin D. Roosevelt, promising massive change, on the way in. But in the meantime, people had to eat, and in Atlanta that was no longer a given.

The word *starving* began to appear routinely in Atlanta newspapers. With the farm economy in ruins, poor blacks and whites streamed into the city, looking for relief. Among the many destitute people in the Atlanta area was a white man who had lost his life's savings in a bank failure and, evicted from his home, dragged his belongs in a wheelbarrow to the woods outside the city, where he was living in a hole he and his seven children had dug in the side of a hill. They drank water from a rain barrel.[1]

Meanwhile, members of a Klan offshoot group calling itself the American Fascisti Organization and Order of Black Shirts marched around Atlanta trumpeting their solution to unemployment: fire black workers until all whites had jobs. They allegedly harassed white employers who hired blacks.[2]

"It is a common expression down here that a white man can be hired cheaper than what it used to cost to hire a negro," Otto Hall, a black Communist and the brother of Harry Haywood, wrote in the *Daily Worker* in the summer of 1932. "Whites are glad to get jobs now that used to be considered exclusively 'nigger jobs.' "[3]

Government relief stations were established to provide shelter and food for the needy and shoes and clothing for children. On one Saturday night, four thousand people were fed at just one Atlanta shelter. A program called "the Penny Club" put collection boxes at theaters and stores, raising $18,000 in donations—1.8 million pennies—to hire people "at a small wage" to maintain city property. The Penny Club also sponsored a separate fund to provide milk for poor children to prevent "a future generation that is under-developed physically and mentally because of malnutrition."[4] A combination of private donations and tax funds paid for many such programs, but it never seemed to be enough.

At the same time, there was an actual program sponsored by the city of Atlanta and the Atlanta Chamber of Commerce to relocate the destitute, in batches of twenty at a time, from the city to rural farms, where they would raise their own food. The participants, called "1932 Pioneers," were provided with homes, land, seed, fertilizer, and farm implements.[5]

The program even offered to move the furniture of the "Pioneers" to their new homes in the country. It was odd that a city or its chamber of commerce would pay to move people out of town, but the poor were seen as huge long-term liabilities. The Pioneers received no salary, just the chance to avoid starvation by applying "elbow grease" on land that was largely abandoned during the Great Depression. It was at best subsistence-level farming. Strangely, the idea had the ring of Soviet farm cooperatives, and the participants—economically, anyway—were little better off than Russian peasants.

"In Atlanta, I never knew when I would be thrown on the street as I had no money for rent," one Pioneer said. "Now at least, I have a roof and no rent collector, a good well, a cow and some land and I'll make my own living before long."[6]

The Atlanta program was racially segregated, like everything else in Southern society. Batches of white and black residents were dispatched to separate farms.

The American Communists saw the back-to-the-farm idea as nothing more than a way to reenslave black people, forcing them either to starve to death or work for room and board only.

Economic conditions continued to deteriorate in Atlanta. That summer, the Fulton County commissioners considered raising property taxes to provide more relief aid to the estimated twenty-two thousand people facing "hunger and destitution."[7]

The problem with raising taxes, however, was that many

property owners, themselves in hard times, couldn't pay their current tax bills, or even the money owed from the year before. The county cut its budget, including the salaries of its employees, but that was just to offset falling property-tax revenue, not for relief money. A prominent citizen named Walter McNeil Jr. stepped forward to say that the back-to-the-farm program, not a tax increase, was the only "concrete solution."

Opponents of the tax increase also criticized what they considered the hefty salaries pulled down by the heads of local charities that were administering county relief grants and raising private donations. One of these was Frank Neely, executive director of the Community Chest, who earned sixty-two hundred dollars a year.

The commissioners took no action on the property-tax increase. The county was out of relief money. It had no more money for the poor.[8]

Little did the commissioners know, but the Communists were in town. Possible death penalties for Herbert Newton and the other members of the Atlanta Six were still pending, but that had not deterred the party from sending activists back to Atlanta.

This time, the leader was a nineteen-year-old Ohio-born black man named Angelo Herndon. Herndon, like many black Communists, had been drawn to the party by racism, abusive capitalism, and the bitter experience when the two were combined. Tall and husky, he was the son of a coal miner who worked ten to fourteen hours a day with little to show for it in the end except a fatal case of black-lung disease—"miner's pneumonia."[9] Herndon's father rarely smiled. "It was overwork, under-nourishment and the burdens of daily living which had made a broken man out of him," Herndon remembered. "His eyes were perpetually inflamed by coal dust which also gnawed away at his lungs and made him spit out black sputum." Religion helped the elder Herndon endure, "distracting him from the sordid realities of his life and that of his family with dreams of the Reward Hearafter."[10]

When Herndon's father died, the family had no money to bury him and had to ask relatives for support. Following the loss of the father's wages, the family was even poorer than before. Herndon's mother worked as a domestic servant for rich whites who mistreated her.

When Herndon was only thirteen, he and his brother left home for Kentucky, where they landed jobs in the coal mines, working ten or eleven hours a day, and sometimes as many as fourteen. They lived in a mine-owned house with no water, toilet, or electricity—but exorbitant rent. They were forced to buy supplies at the company store. Their jobs were grueling, dangerous, and low paying.

At the same time, Herndon had to deal with racism. Like Benjamin Mays and so many other black people of that era, he had been lectured by his parents "never to get excited, always to be humble and patient in the face of white brutality, to turn my gaze to the Lamb of God."

It was while working in a coal mine in Birmingham, Alabama, that Herndon was radicalized. He joined the Communist Party and eventually made the grade of paid organizer. Before being transferred to Atlanta, he tried to recruit sharecroppers in Alabama, rallying support for the Scottsboro defendants.

He was living in a boardinghouse and earning $10 a

week—$520 a year—when Fulton County announced that it was out of relief money.[11]

Herndon helped organize a rally on June 30 at the Fulton County Courthouse, distributing ten thousand fliers under cover of darkness to mailboxes throughout the city under the name of the Unemployed Committee of Atlanta, P.O. Box 339, and addressed to "Workers of Atlanta, Negro and White."

The "miserable" relief payments had been halted, and thousands of people now faced starvation and eviction, according to the handout. "The bosses want us to starve peacefully," said the flier, which mentioned Neely's salary of sixty-two hundred dollars a year and the back-to-the-farm solution.[12]

Herndon was effective in drawing a crowd. An estimated 400 blacks and 150 whites, including mothers with babies in their arms, gathered on the courthouse steps on a Thursday morning, demanding help.[13] The demonstrators then crowded into the courthouse outside the fifth-floor offices of the county commissioners. After waiting thirty minutes in the hallway, only the white demonstrators were allowed to enter the office of county commissioner Walter Stewart, who fell back on the back-to-the-farm solution, suggesting that anyone with relatives still living on the land should consider migrating back there. The county, he said, would even consider providing transportation out of town. The times were that desperate.

But the Communist-organized protest, particularly its biracial makeup, rattled Fulton County elected officials, who the very next day somehow managed to find six thousand dollars in relief money, which they spent at a wholesale grocery to purchase food for the poor.[14]

The demonstrators had won the first round, but the fight did not end there. One of the county commissioners, not appreciating the ambush, asked a Fulton County prosecutor, E. A. Stephens, to investigate the source of the "scurrilous" fliers announcing the rally. Stephens requested that the police stake out P.O. Box 339.[15]

Flush with victory, Herndon casually walked into the post office on the night of July 10 to check his mail at P.O. Box 339. Two Atlanta detectives arrested him the second he opened it. They seized a batch of pamphlets in the P.O. box and in Herndon's satchel and then asked the teenager to take them to his home. He first led the detectives to a house on Coleman Street, but a black man living there said he didn't know Herndon. It was then on to Hubbard Street, where a woman named Carrie Jackson said that, yes, Herndon boarded there. The police then searched Herndon's room, which was filled with boxes of "newspapers, books, periodicals and such."[16]

This Communist literature was much more radical than the material Herbert Newton and the Atlanta Six had been distributing two years earlier in Atlanta when they were arrested. The idea of a separate black nation in the South had evolved from a concept to an actual shaded map, the territory stretching from Arkansas and Louisiana east through Mississippi, Alabama, Georgia, and Florida.

In this new state, the land of white farmers would be confiscated, the documents said. The new Black Belt state would determine "ITSELF the relations between its country and other governments, especially the United States."[17]

The documents stressed that this idea for a new state

was not theoretical. At some point would come an "uprising." In the meantime, there were to be "mass actions, such as demonstrations, strikes, tax boycott movements." This would be a "NATIONAL REBELLION."[18]

Also found in the documents were receipts for new Communists recruited by Herndon and for donations given to the Communist Party candidates for president and vice president in the 1932 election, William Z. Foster and James Ford, a black man from Alabama. According to the seized documents, membership dues for the party were ten cents a week for anyone earning less than fifteen dollars a week, rising to a dollar a week for those who made up to fifty dollars a week. There was a special surcharge for those above the fifty-dollars-per-week threshold.[19]

Herndon "confessed" to police that, while in Atlanta, he had recruited five new party members and had held several meetings to drum up support for the cause. The minutes of those meetings were also seized.[20]

It was not illegal to be a Communist, as evidenced by the fact that two party members, Foster and Ford, were on the ballot in the 1932 presidential election. Even so, Herndon, like Herbert Newton and other members of the Atlanta Six, was indicted for attempted insurrection, which in Georgia was defined as trying "to induce others to join in combined resistance to the lawful authority of the state of Georgia."[21] This was the Reconstruction-era law that had been written to prevent former Confederates from rebelling against Georgia's government, which then included blacks and Northern "carpetbaggers."[22]

Herndon, like Newton and the Atlanta Six, faced death in the electric chair if convicted.

While prosecutors had been in no rush to bring the Atlanta Six to trial, that was not the case with Herndon. He was a lone black man who was too successful, too close to the flame, for comfort. Herndon had created a biracial uprising in storming the courthouse. And the teenager had achieved real results, putting food in the mouths of starving people, an accomplishment the Communists were touting as they moved on to even larger demonstrations.

Whereas the Atlanta Six were all out on bond within six weeks, Herndon would spend more than two years in the medieval-looking jail known as Fulton Towers, in part because authorities initially set his bail at twenty-five thousand dollars, triple that of the Atlanta Six. It was later lowered to twenty-five hundred, allowing Herndon only a brief respite from jail until his trial began in January.

International Labor Defense hired two black Atlanta attorneys, Benjamin Davis Jr. and John Geer, to represent Herndon.

Davis was a tall, affable Harvard Law School graduate who had attended Morehouse College for high school because Atlanta had no black high schools at the time. He had gone on to play football at Amherst, where he received his undergraduate degree before attending Harvard. Davis was from a prosperous family in Atlanta. His father owned a local black newspaper, the *Atlanta Independent*, and was a leader in a black fraternal organization, the Grand United Order of Odd Fellows in America (as distinct from the Independent Order of Odd Fellows). The elder Davis was a prominent Republican who had controlled the federal patronage jobs in Atlanta in the 1920s era of Calvin Coolidge and Herbert Hoover, much to the dismay of white job seekers.[23]

As Herndon's attorney, Ben Davis Jr. immediately challenged the total absence of blacks on the grand jury that indicted his client, calling as witnesses members of the Fulton County Jury Commission, who could not remember any black on any local grand jury stretching back decades. The only blacks qualified to serve on grand juries were professional men such as doctors and lawyers, and they were exempt from service, one jury commissioner testified. Rarely were blacks chosen, either, for the regular trial jury pool.[24]

When that objection was overruled, Davis sought to ask each prospective juror in the Herndon case, all of whom were white men, whether or not race prejudice would influence his decision. Judge Lee Wyatt would not allow that line of questioning. Wyatt would go on to become a justice of the Georgia Supreme Court.

Herndon's trial lasted only three days. No witness could testify to seeing Herndon actually distributing the Communist pamphlets, only that they were in his possession. It was Herndon's "confession" of holding recruitment meetings around town that was the prosecution's key evidence of attempted insurrection.

Taking the witness stand for the prosecution, E. A. Stephens, the assistant solicitor, recalled interviewing "this darkey, Angelo Herndon," shortly after police arrested him.[25]

Davis jumped up to object. "Mr. Stephens refers to the defendant as 'darkey,'" he said. "Your Honor, we wish to remind the prosecution if they insist on using such opprobrious terms to the defendant, we will have to ask for a mistrial, because it's prejudicial to our case."

The judge replied to Stephens, "I don't know whether it is or isn't, but suppose you refer to him as the defendant."

Stephens didn't comply with the judge's request. "I will refer to him as Negro, which is better," Stephens said. "He is the darkey with glasses on in the middle."[26]

Davis did not make a motion for a mistrial despite the repeated use of the word *darkey*.

For the defense, Davis called an Emory University economics professor, Mercer G. Evans, trying to make the point that the materials Herndon possessed were no more radical than books—such as works by Lenin and Marx—available in local libraries, including Emory's. The judge nixed much of the questioning, commenting that it was irrelevant to the Herndon case. "If Emory University is guilty of anything, we will try them," Wyatt said. "It is a question of what the defendant's done."[27]

Davis tried again with another Emory professor, T. J. Corley, who was sympathetic with some aspects of the Communists' proposals, including unemployment insurance and emergency relief for farmers.

On cross-examination, Corley was questioned about the Communists' position on equal rights for blacks. "You understand that to mean the right of a colored boy to marry your daughter, if you have one?" assistant prosecutor Roy LeCraw asked.[28]

It had finally surfaced, the obsession that was so prevalent, particularly in Southern society, over sex between white women and black men.

Davis immediately objected, telling the judge that the Communist Party's platform on racial intermarriage was not an issue in Herndon's trial and in fact had never been mentioned until now by anyone. Wyatt overruled the objection.

"A negro doesn't have the right to marry my daughter

under the laws of this state," Corley reminded LeCraw.

"Did you know that there are 20 states in the United States where the two races can intermarry or mix?" LeCraw continued.

Again, Davis objected. Again, Wyatt overruled. But the mere mention of miscegenation was damming to Herndon, Davis would later say, and could only "inflame the minds of the jury and divert their minds from the material issues of facts."

At the climax of the trial, Herndon took the stand to give an unsworn statement, which by Georgia law was exempt from cross-examination. The young man spoke to the jury for thirty minutes, rambling but passionate.[29]

After nearly six months in jail, he complained about the food and the lack of medical care for prisoners. He complained of being locked in a small cell with a dead inmate. Jailers never denied that, though they did dispute how long it took undertakers to remove the body.

But the real theme of Herndon's speech was that racism was designed to divide black and white workers, to pit them against each other and distract them from challenging the ruling class. That was precisely the reason, Herndon told the jury, that county commissioner Walter Stewart had immediately divided the white and black demonstrators who crowded the courthouse and agreed to meet only with the whites. It was also why, despite insisting there was no more money for relief, the county somehow found six thousand dollars the very next day.

"In order for white workers to get relief, and in order for black workers to get relief, they will have to get together and forget about this question of racial discrimination," Herndon told the jurors. "Forget about this question of the white skin and the black skin because both are starving and the Capitalistic Class will continue to prey on this tune of racial discrimination; that the negro skin is black and yours white and therefore the negro is no good."

Repeatedly, Herndon told the jurors that the fight for equality would not end with him. "I can say this quite clearly," he stated. "There will be more Angelo Herndons to come in the future, because of the fact there are thousands of negro workers starving and there are thousands of white workers starving."

In closing arguments to the jury, the lead prosecutor in this case, John Hudson, a lay preacher, waved his arms and spoke passionately. With tears in his eyes, he asked the jurors to "send this damnable anarchist Bolsheviki to death by electrocution."[30]

In his closing, Davis described in detail the horrible lynching of a pregnant black woman. So vivid was the description that one of the courtroom spectators fainted. "Gentlemen of the jury, it is not Herndon who is the insurrectionist," Davis said. "It is the lynch mobs, the Ku Kluxers who are allowed to roam the land of this state burning innocent black people at the stake in defiance of every law of justice, humanity and right."[31]

Davis was hopeful when the jurors took nearly three hours to reach a verdict. They found Herndon guilty but recommended mercy, meaning he would not be executed in the electric chair. Still, the jury recommended a sentence of eighteen to twenty years, which on the brutal Georgia chain gang was for many inmates effectively a death sentence.

Robert Burns, the disenchanted World War I veteran

who had returned home expecting a hero's welcome but instead found himself unable to land a job, ended up on the Georgia chain gang for a robbery that netted nine dollars. In 1932, he published a book—*I Am a Fugitive from a Georgia Chain Gang!*—that later became a Hollywood movie. Burns described the horrors of Georgia's system: roused by guards at three-thirty in the morning, manual labor under the hot sun until six at night, beatings with bullwhips by sadistic guards.[32]

This was the life Herndon faced for the next two decades. His lawyers, of course, would appeal. The Communists, as they had in the Scottsboro case, counted on the appellate system and the Constitution to deliver justice.

After announcing Herndon's sentence, Wyatt, who would later sit in judgment on former Nazis at the Nuremburg trials, called twenty years of incarceration for Herndon "thoroughly justifiable."

The *St. Louis Post Dispatch* called the sentence "shameful."[33]

But what did Herndon do that was illegal? He possessed inflammatory Communist literature, yes, but no witness saw him actually distribute the pamphlets. In his charge to the jury, Wyatt said that "mere possession" of the literature was not enough to warrant a conviction. The judge also advised the jurors that engaging in "academic or philosophic discussions, however radical or revolutionary in their nature," would not be enough to convict Herndon.[34]

Georgia's laws, Wyatt said, made it illegal to "attempt by persuasion to induce others to join in resistance to the lawful authority of the state," and this had to be "manifested or intended to be manifested by acts of violence."

Herndon had recruited a handful of new members to the

Communist Party, which was a legal entity in the United States. But the courthouse demonstration was by all accounts non-violent, and its goal was food for the hungry, not overthrow of the government. Long-term, the Communists very much wanted to install their own regime in the United States. But what about the here and now?

Was Herndon in fact a political prisoner?

That was what the appellate courts would have to decide.

Again, Georgia had created a Communist celebrity, fodder for headlines and propaganda worldwide. Petitions supporting Herndon would pour into Atlanta, one purportedly containing two million signatures.

Although he was not immediately sent to the chain gang, Herndon would spend another twenty-seven months in jail in Fulton County, on top of the six months he had already served, before the Communists could raise his bail, set at fifteen thousand dollars at that point. Herbert Newton had spent six weeks in the Fulton jail and was able to joke about it as a "vacation." Herndon's sentence was no joke, no vacation.

Meanwhile, his lawyer, Benjamin Davis Jr., could not take it anymore. The Harvard Law School graduate, son of a prominent Atlanta family, officially joined the Communist Party while Herndon's trial was still under way.

"I was at 29 years old, sure of the Marxist outlook as the path of liberation of the Negro people," Davis would later write.[35]

He would devote the rest of his life to the Communist cause.

CHAPTER 6

Sanity TRIAL

Perhaps Georgia prosecutors were now satiated. Perhaps twenty years on the chain gang for Angelo Herndon would be the pound of Communist flesh that would convince the party to stay away from the Deep South.

Or maybe Herndon's conviction and stiff sentence would only encourage Georgia to go ahead and pursue the Atlanta Six.

Herbert Newton, living in Chicago and still in a relationship with Jane, had no way of knowing what Georgia's next move would be or whether or not he, like Herndon, would end up with a long sentence on the chain gang. But Newton did not let Herndon's arrest and conviction intimidate him. Instead, he ran for Congress in the pivotal election of 1932 that would change the course of America.[1]

Newton was the Communist Party challenger to First District congressman Oscar De Priest, a Republican and the only black member of Congress. The very thought of De Priest rankled the South. When President Herbert Hoover entertained De Priest's wife at the White House in 1929, the Mississippi State Senate had officially objected, saying this threatened the "integrity of the white race."[2]

The Communists were also no fans of De Priest, believing him to be a capitalist sellout, not a black pioneer. In July, fifteen hundred Communists demonstrated outside the congressman's office at Thirty-fifth Street and Wabash Avenue in Chicago. They demanded to know why De Priest had not spoken out on the Scottsboro case and why he voted against bonuses for World War I veterans. Communists threw bricks at police, and the police clubbed demonstrators.[3]

As the November election approached, the congressman had just completed a speech at Blackwell Memorial Church at Oakwood Boulevard and Langley Avenue when Newton jumped up from his seat in the audience and demanded that De Priest explain his position on Scottsboro and soldier bonuses.[4] These were classic agitprop tactics.

"Sit down," De Priest said. "I'll answer."

But the Communists would not allow the congressman to respond. They rose "as if by signal and commenced heckling. The congressman tried to answer but his words were drowned out by the noise." Other speakers attempted to quiet the crowd, but the Communists started swearing and "bedlam ensued." Two Communists, "badly bruised" in a fight with police, were arrested and charged with disorderly conduct, unlawful assembly, and inciting a riot.

The next week, Newton led an estimated twenty-five thousand people in a peaceful demonstration in the Chicago Loop, the red flag of the Soviet Union waving on Michigan

Avenue and a thousand police officers ready in case of trouble. The protesters objected to a planned 50 percent cut in relief aid. The situation in Chicago was not as dire as in Atlanta, where all relief had been temporarily suspended the previous summer, but it was severe nevertheless. Newton's demands were sweeping: relief cash payments lowered no further than to $7.50 a week for a family of three, free natural gas and water, an end to evictions and foreclosures, city-built homes for the poor, unemployment insurance, and release of all prisoners arrested in demonstrations.[5]

For De Priest, the real challenge was not Newton or the Communists but his white Democratic opponent, Harry Baker. A Democratic landslide was in the making, starting at the top of the ticket with Franklin D. Roosevelt and extending to state and local offices nationwide. De Priest managed to hold on to his seat, in part with white GOP support, defeating Baker by six thousand votes.

Herbert Newton attracted only 903 votes.[6] Nationally, the Communist ticket of William Z. Foster and James Ford received only 103,314 votes despite the worst economic crisis in American history. FDR received more than 22 million votes. The ballot box was not proving to be a successful venue for the Communists, who had not been able to generate a mass following even after being handed a gift in the form of the Great Depression.

And this was before the massive New Deal programs kicked in that directed hundreds of millions of dollars in relief aid to the poor. There would also be government jobs programs, laws against child labor and for union organization, Social Security payments for the elderly, and public housing for the poor.

Other than universal health care, these were all major components of the Communist agenda, delivered by someone else, namely FDR. It caught the American Communists flatfooted and speechless. Should they oppose the New Deal or support it? They weren't quite sure.

Earl Browder, head of the American Communist Party, actually "despised" FDR for "stealing the working class from the workers' parties," wrote Browder's biographer, James Ryan.[7]

Georgi Dimitrov, a high-ranking Communist leader and head of the party's international wing, publicly berated the American Communists in 1935 for criticizing FDR. The Communists were increasingly worried about the Nazis and fascism, and Dimitrov flatly told the Americans that only "a confirmed idiot" would fail to see that it was members of the pro-Nazi American financial sector who were FDR's strongest critics. Humiliated, Browder, "swiftly changed his outlook on FDR," Ryan wrote.[8]

The New Deal's sweeping programs stabilized the economy and probably prevented an outright revolution. But they did not eliminate America's race problems, which would continue to fester long after the Great Depression ended.

In 1933, Jane became pregnant with Newton's child. Although she was still estranged from her family, the pregnancy prompted a visit from her parents. Jane's mother did not approve of her interracial relationship with Herbert but could not bring herself to criticize her daughter. Despite their many disagreements, Jane's mother "perceived at once that I was happier than I had been for a long time," Jane wrote.[9]

Jane and Herbert married in September 1933, and their

daughter was born on Thanksgiving Day. Had their firstborn been a boy, they would have named him Karl in honor of Karl Marx. Instead, Herbert and Jane settled for Michelle, after Louise Michel, a leader of the revolutionary Paris commune that had ruled Paris for more than a month in 1871. Michel was "an inspiring figure whose life could be a guide for her namesake," Jane said.[10]

Jane and Herbert lived on the South Side of Chicago. They were poor but happy, surviving on relief payments, just like many millions at the time, waiting for the Great Depression to loosen its grip. The Newtons' only luxury was a phonograph, upon which they played Bach, Beethoven, and operas. When Herbert wasn't working, he liked to read and play chess.

The South Side at the time was a "wasteland of decaying buildings in which lived thousands and thousands of negro people, jobless, fed mostly from leftover supplies from bankrupt warehouses, thin-shoed, threadbare, forgotten, it seemed by the rest of the world," Jane would later recall with her writer's descriptive flair.[11]

The life of a revolutionary was not a glamorous one. "Many people imagine that communists go around plotting, sneaking, making bombs and inciting violence," Jane wrote. "Quite the contrary. Our occupations were teaching and speaking with people in the neighborhood. No change will be possible until the majority of the people feel that a change is necessary. It will be communist-led change only if we are able to show how socialism will benefit society."[12]

It was an impoverished life, but also an intellectual one, electrified by books, ideas, music, art, poetry, and political debate. It was in this world that Jane and Herbert met young

Communist writer Richard Wright, who had joined the mass migration of blacks from the Deep South to Chicago, looking for a better life.

Wright had first moved from Mississippi to Memphis, where his father abandoned the family. After his mother suffered a series of strokes, Wright found himself the sole breadwinner, dropping out of school after the eighth grade to find work. In that regard, his story was similar to those of many other young Communists at the time, including Herbert Newton, Angelo Herndon, Anne Burlak, and Mary Licht. They had experienced firsthand a world without safety nets and knew the bare-knuckled struggle to feed a family, to survive day to day.

It was not surprising that Communism would prove attractive to these young people, given its promise of jobs, health care, retirement, and, as an added bonus, an end to racial discrimination. Jane was, of course, an anomaly, born to a prominent, wealthy family, with no worries about where her next meal was coming from. Yet here she was on the South Side of Chicago, a poor white Communist amid a sea of black faces. Despite her background, she had somehow transcended traditional white views on race and capitalism. For her, Communism was not just a theory in a book. She could have chosen the life of a Park Avenue Communist, donating cash to the cause. But instead, she was living the life among the people the party was trying to help and recruit.

Would-be writers such as Wright saw one other major advantage of Communism: the chance to get published in party publications. In Chicago, Wright joined the local chapter of the John Reed Club, a Communist organization of writers and artists.

Jane was not a member of the John Reed Club, but she

and Herbert met Wright once he became a full-fledged Communist Party member. Wright was at the time a "slim, fresh-faced young man. He smiled often when he spoke, his voice softly shaded with tones of the speech of the Mississippi basin."[13]

It was through the John Reed Club that Wright published his first poetry, in the group's *Left Front* magazine. The club also introduced him to his first, but surely not his last, dose of Communist infighting: the painters versus the writers. The writers nominated Wright to chair the Chicago branch of the club, knowing that the painters could not vote against a black man at a time when the party was desperately trying to recruit black members. Wright thought he was being used by the white members. It was a theme that would resurface later as Wright gained fame as a writer.

Meanwhile, the Newtons suddenly found themselves dealing with the reality of Northern racism. Typically, landlords were reluctant to rent to interracial couples even in the North. There were ways around this, as Jane and Herbert would discover. Depending on the race of the landlord, either Jane or Herbert would sign the lease alone, the other arriving at the apartment later, after all the paperwork had been completed.

In December 1934, Jane and Herbert were subletting part of an apartment at 615 Oakwood Boulevard from a white woman named Harriet Williams. Newton was the only black tenant in the building. This was an Irish Catholic neighborhood, but one that in the 1930s was slowly in transition as blacks migrated to Chicago from the Deep South. Whites were trying to stave off the inevitable.[14]

Businessmen in the area and some parishioners at nearby Holy Angels Catholic Church complained to the apartment building's owner, Dr. O. L. Mitchell, who told Harriet Williams either to evict the Newtons or move out. She refused. Mitchell filed papers in Chicago's "Renters' Court" to have Williams and the Newtons evicted.[15]

The white tenants in the apartment building didn't want Newton evicted. They signed a petition calling it persecution "based solely on the fact that Mr. Newton happens to be a Negro."

The case landed on the desk of a white judge, an ex-marine named Thomas A. Green, who gave Williams just five days to vacate the apartment. The Communist-affiliated International Labor Defense entered the case on behalf of Williams. Supporters were baffled as to what legal authority Green had to order the eviction. It was not illegal to sublet an apartment to a black person, and Williams was not behind on her rent. Evictions were rampant virtually everywhere in the United States during the Great Depression, and ending them was a key part of the Communist agenda. But the dispute over Herbert Newton's residency was not about money at all. It was about race.

On a cold, rainy Chicago day in mid-December, bailiffs arrived at the apartment building and tossed all the Newtons' furniture, including the cherished phonograph, on the sidewalk. Harriet Williams also was evicted. Friends of Jane and Herbert helped them move their belongings back into the apartment, an act of civil disobedience and nonviolent militant resistance—militant in that it defied the government's authority. There is no indication that this was a planned event by the Communists, but it nevertheless created a reaction greater than an organized march.

Police promptly arrested Jane and Herbert and charged

them with disorderly conduct. Jane soon found herself before Judge Green, who sentenced her to pay a two-hundred-dollar fine, money she did not have. It was off to jail for both Jane and Herbert, who was also fined two hundred dollars and also did not have the money to pay.[16] Twenty-six-year-old Jane, described by newspaper reporters as "slender" and "drably dressed," was chain-smoking cigarettes and was "apparently unembarrassed by her situation."[17]

As Jane was being escorted to jail, a lawyer in the courtroom, Marvin J. Bas, recognized her. Bas was a former high-school classmate from Grand Rapids. Jane acknowledged Bas, who then approached the bench and told Judge Green who Jane was: the daughter of former American Legion commander John Emery.

"This is a terrible example of what happens when adolescent students listen to communist teachings," the judge said. "Parents who make sacrifices to school their children should have some assurance that the universities will prevent loose-minded professors from inculcating them with wild-minded ideas."[18]

The judge spared Jane from jail but in a surprise move ordered her to undergo a psychiatric evaluation, on the obvious premise that a daughter of such a prominent white family would have to be insane to turn her back on such an upbringing to marry a black Communist.

"I'm to be considered not quite right in my senses for my marriage and the communist principles I profess," Jane told a newspaper reporter. "Well, alright, that's the way they look at it."

In questioning Jane's sanity, Green was ahead of the Soviet Union by decades in using psychiatry as punishment for dissidents. It was not until the 1970s that the Soviets resorted to these tactics. At the same time, Jane was decades ahead of her time in her views on race, compared to most American whites.

Judge Green's views on women were typical of the times, as reflected in the various cases that came before him in court, including that of a drugstore employee who said he beat his wife with a strap to keep her from staying out all night. The wife offered to show Green the welts, but the judge sent the couple home with this advice: "True love never runs smoothly."

It was clear that Jane had touched a nerve with Judge Green. She evoked a response that was different, and in some ways more severe, than Georgia's reaction to Herbert Newton and Angelo Herndon, who had been handled as mere criminals, not lunatics. It was understandable that black men such as Newton and Herndon would be attracted to Communism or any other lifeboat that promised to end racism. Even the Mary Lichts and Anne Burlaks of the world were considered misguided but not crazy, emerging as they did from the lower ranks of white society. Not so Jane, who had a war-hero father. Jane represented the threat that Communism had infiltrated not just the margins of society but the mainstream.

Her attendance at a major university, the University of Michigan, was further evidence that the Communists were coming in through college campuses. A member of the Chicago Police Department's "Red Squad," which investigated Communists, recalled seeing Jane marching in a Communist protest wearing a cap and gown, encouraging college students to join the cause.[19]

"The condition in which this woman finds herself is the

outgrowth of what they permit to be taught in the universities," said Lloyd D. Heth, a leader in the anti-Communist movement and a prosecutor in the 1920 Chicago trial of twenty-one Communists convicted of trying to overthrow the United States government, a harbinger of future crackdowns on American Communists.

An additional factor was the underlying fear that the Communists were using attractive young white women as "bait" for black Communists. Although this was not true in Jane's case, the public didn't know that. The real trouble white society had with Jane, which had surfaced in the Angelo Herndon trial in Atlanta as well, was the whole idea of whites marrying blacks—miscegenation—which the Communists accepted but did not necessarily encourage.

While Herbert Newton remained in jail, Jane was examined by David R. Rotman, psychiatric director of Chicago Municipal Court. Rotman would turn out to have what would now be considered bizarre views on women, his biases reflected in his psychiatry. For example, he concluded that women who received large inheritances became "psychologically crippled parasites."[20] His study of seventy-one "ritzy moochers" found that, after blowing the money left to them by their late husbands, the women became dependent on their friends in a form of "high-toned begging much more vicious and deteriorating than the out-and-out street begging type." Equal rights were turning women into alcoholics, Rotman also warned. "They seem to think they have equal rights to drinking as well as to jobs," he explained.[21]

Rotman quickly diagnosed Jane as having "simple schizophrenia" and ordered her committed to the Cook County Psychopathic Hospital.[22] "Her communist sentiments are part of her mania," Rotman said. "Her defiance of accepted social conduct indicates a cause fixation and her peculiar addiction is the equality of the races, socially, economically and sexually."[23]

Although Jane was estranged from her father, John Emery hired Bas to represent her. International Labor Defense also sent lawyers.

At the psychopathic hospital, two psychiatrists—one of them Clarence Neymann, who had been a defense witness in the infamous Leopold and Loeb murder trial—agreed with Rotman that Jane was indeed mentally ill. Francis Gerty, the second psychiatrist, concluded that Jane "must be suffering from some mental ailment, but I wish to approach the matter with an open mind." By "throwing herself at this Negro," Jane was displaying a self-sacrificing pattern of going "beneath her station," Gerty said.[24]

While she was in the hospital, Jane received a letter from a citizen who called her "worse than a cannibal" for marrying Newton.[25]

White American society's obsession over whether blacks and whites were having sex or getting married was not on trial here, nor was white racism, which then as now was considered by psychiatry to be a learned behavior taught by the culture, not an organic condition. Yet somehow, psychiatrists could deem it insane not to be a racist.

"How strangely curious are the ways of the Superior Sane!" wrote Dewey Jones, a black writer for the *Chicago Defender* newspaper.[26]

Robert S. Abbott, editor of the *Defender*, could not help pointing out the hypocrisy that white men having sex with black women was rarely questioned or criticized by white society, particularly in the South. "It is all right for white men to satisfy their passion in nauseating and unholy concub[in]age, but when a black takes on a white woman in a state of holy matrimony, then a great crime has been committed," Abbott wrote.[27]

Neymann and Gerty were overruled by the findings of two other psychiatrists, Sydney Kuh, who worked at the hospital, and Aaron Learner, hired by Jane's defense team. Kuh was emphatic after a ninety-minute discussion with Jane. "It is my opinion that she is not only sane but is distinctly above the average in intelligence," he testified at the sanity hearing on December 19. Learner found Jane "well oriented and well composed. She has made certain decisions that are not regular perhaps but not psychiatric."[28]

Judge Win G. Knoch, presiding over the county's "Psychopathic Court," released Jane after four days in a mental hospital.

"All I want is to be left alone with my husband and baby," Jane said. "I want to rebuild my life. It's like a ruined anthill."[29]

She felt vindicated by the outcome of the sanity hearing. "The court's decision seems to have proved that a person's political beliefs are hardly evidence enough to send him or her to an insane asylum," Jane wrote.[30]

In their prosecution of Jane, the Chicago authorities had created another Communist hero and given the party a huge agitprop victory and headlines around the world. But Jane did not appear to relish the spotlight. This was familiar territory for Herbert Newton, trained as he was in hardcore agitprop, used to getting arrested and even beaten by police. Jane had been swept up in all this suddenly and seemed worn and frazzled by it all.

In the sanity hearing, Judge Knoch asked Jane, "Do you believe your example if followed would help the world?"

"No," Jane replied nearly inaudibly. "My life as it stands is not an example. I have tried but I have made many mistakes."

She deeply regretted the pain and embarrassment the case had inflicted on her parents, who had stood by her in providing legal help despite their disapproval of her marriage and political views.

"I am calling to say how sorry I am that all this happened," Jane told her mother in a phone call to Grand Rapids. "I would have, if it had been possible, kept any mention of my family name out of court entirely. I hope you will feel this was not my fault."[31]

"Yes, yes, I understand, dear," her mother replied.

"Give Daddy my love," Jane ended the call. "Goodbye, Mother dear."

The day after her release, a still "shabbily dressed" Jane received a hero's welcome at the Madison Street offices of International Labor Defense. "They swarmed around her, colored and white," a reporter wrote. "Everywhere it was 'Jane.' They patted her on the back. They lit their cigarettes from hers, they grasped her hands, both of them."

Asked by the reporter if she would continue to be a Communist, Jane waved her cigarette, pointing to the people around her of both races.

"These are my people," she said.[32]

CHAPTER 7

Back to RUSSIA

For a while after Jane was judged sane, she was in the national spotlight, giving speeches and becoming a published writer with an autobiographical series of essays in the *Chicago Times* newspaper.

Herbert continued his job as a Communist agitator and journalist, a double celebrity now, first as a member of the Atlanta Six and now for the infamous eviction case. Herbert continued to organize protests and to get arrested, which was basically his job description. He also continued to run unsuccessfully for public office, this time for Chicago city clerk.

In March 1935, he was arrested in Chicago along with Jack Kling, twenty-one-year-old secretary of the Young Communist League, after they refused police orders to abandon a street demonstration. Kling's trial attracted an interesting witness for the defense, a twenty-two-year-old white

University of Chicago student named Virginia Bash, whose father was United States Army general and quartermaster Louis H. Bash.[1] Virginia Bash had attended the Communist rally and testified that she was very much interested in learning more about the movement, which was a "much discussed topic" on the University of Chicago campus. The university would reprimand Virginia for writing that it had the "wrong attitude" toward blacks on campus.[2] Perhaps Jane's critics were justified in fearing that the Communists were making inroads, as yet another daughter of prominence had defected to the other side.

Later that month, Jane and Herbert spoke at Mount Olive Baptist Church in Detroit. The next night, they were feted at a YMCA banquet at which Angelo Herndon, out on bond awaiting appeal of his Georgia conviction, also spoke.

More than two hundred people, 40 percent of them white, attended the banquet, but the YMCA took heat for inviting the Newtons. It was "bombarded" with phone calls and even personal visits from opponents of interracial marriage. The *Detroit Times*, a Hearst paper, didn't seem to appreciate the Newtons' trip to town either, noting that the couple spoke "disparagingly" of government officials, including President Roosevelt.[3]

After the eviction case, the Newtons seemed to be moving up in the world. In January 1934, Judge Green lifted Jane's probation for disorderly conduct after the couple removed their furniture from the Oakwood Boulevard apartment. The Newtons rented a much larger apartment at the corner of Forty-eighth Street and Prairie Avenue in Chicago's Bronzeville neighborhood. Jane was pregnant with their second child, a boy. Jane and Herbert would finally have their

Karl, who—ironically, considering the drama Jane had experienced in late 1934—would go on to become a psychiatrist.

At the new apartment, Richard Wright, now a published poet thanks to Communist Party publications, became a closer friend. "Frequently, he would have manuscripts in his pocket to read to us," Jane would recall decades later. "The apartment was large and became a place to drop in for coffee and talk for students, musicians, relief investigators, 'in the field' communists, all kinds of people who would listen if Dick [Wright] or some other person would have something to read or say."[4]

Aspiring novelist Meyer Levin, who was white, and future playwright Ted Ward, who was black, were also among the visitors to the Newtons' apartment, a salon for writers and other artists.

Wright clicked with Herbert and Jane Newton and other well-educated members of the Communist Party. But the rank-and-file members weren't sure quite what to make of him.

Each Communist was assigned to a "unit" that met regularly and secretly to pay dues, to hear the party's take on world events, and to be assigned tasks. At his first unit meeting, Wright, wearing a shirt and tie and shined shoes, introduced himself to the group, describing his work as a writer in the John Reed Club. There was complete silence from the other comrades. Then Wright noticed that they were all trying as hard as they could to suppress their laughter. Within a few minutes, they could no longer control their amusement. "He talks like a book," one member later commented.[5]

Wright, who had only an eighth-grade education, was shocked to learn that many of his fellow Communists viewed him as an intellectual, a kiss of death in the party of the workers. Most black Communists at the time had even less education than Wright. Many were "functional illiterates," Jane recalled. For them, *intellectual* meant "being able to read and write easily," she wrote.[6]

Wright denied that he was an intellectual. But Jane sensed that "he would not mind being one," although he wasn't quite there yet. It could well have been Wright's pretentiousness that his fellow Communists found so amusing.

The grandson of slaves and the son of a Mississippi sharecropper, Wright was largely self-educated, and an avid reader of books. He sensed that the party was exploiting uneducated Southern blacks who had migrated to Chicago in search of a better life. They could barely read or write and could therefore not examine for themselves the pros and cons of Communism. They could not really question the party line.

"I found that they were not vicious," Wright said. "They just did not know anything and did not want to learn anything. They felt all questions had been answered and anyone who asked new ones was dangerous."

Wright and the Communists started off on the wrong foot, and it only got worse.

He was once holding a book under his arm and a comrade asked, "What're you reading it for?"

"It's interesting," said Wright.

"Reading bourgeois books can only confuse you, comrade," said the other Communist.

"Didn't Lenin read bourgeois books?"

"But you're not Lenin."[7]

Wright really angered his fellow Communists when

he proposed to write biographical sketches of some of his more interesting comrades, including a black man from the South named David R. Poindexter. "Dex" was married to a white woman and dared to publicly speak out on the merits of Communism. "He was a slim, dark fellow with a volatile disposition and a ready flow of speech," Jane wrote. "Dex liked to speak on street corners even in situations where it would be dangerous to do so. I have seen him in a meeting, his words never stopping until a policeman took him by the collar and cracked his head as if it were an egg."[8]

Poindexter had been one of the two men arrested in the 1932 melee that erupted when Herbert Newton was challenging Oscar De Priest for Congress and confronted De Priest at Blackwell Memorial Church. In May 1934, Poindexter was one of six Communists, two of them women, convicted on charges resulting from another brawl, this one outside the unemployment relief station at 505 East Fiftieth Street the previous January. This was another demonstration turned violent, both protesters and police officers ending up bruised and bandaged, one policeman actually stabbed. When Poindexter could not be found after the riot, journalists speculated he was so badly beaten that he had to be taken to the hospital, a charge that police denied.[9]

Poindexter was in fact becoming too radical for the party, which was trying to broaden its support by reaching out to other groups, including churches. Poindexter loudly disagreed with the strategy, and Wright suffered from his association with the man, even though Jane would later write that it was actually Poindexter's right to disagree with the party line that Wright was defending. Even so, the Chicago Communists were increasingly suspicious of Wright's motives, fearing he was gathering information for the police. Again, they branded Wright with the label *intellectual*.

Wright was one of many restless young black men on the South Side of Chicago during the Great Depression, wearing worn shoes and relying on government relief assistance while desperately trying to make a living. He sold burial insurance door to door to poor black people, supporting his mother and brother while also trying to become a writer, a goal his family members considered to be a "frittering away of time." In that same period, he found a relief job at the Chicago Boys Club that allowed him to temporarily make ends meet.

As the Communists became more distrustful of Wright, he was summoned to the apartment of Harry Haywood, the black Communist who had studied in Moscow with Herbert Newton and had been the first African American to support self-determination for blacks in the South. Haywood was now head of the "Negro Department" of the American Communist Party, based in Chicago. He was a big deal in the party.

Haywood was a "short, black man with an ever ready smile, thick lips, a furtive manner and a greasy, sweaty look," Wright said. "Now and then he would punctuate his words by taking a nip of whiskey."[10]

Although Wright recognized Haywood's status in the Communist Party not just in the United States but internationally, he was not impressed. "I thought I would encounter a man of ideas, but he was not that," Wright said. "Then, perhaps he was man of action? But he was not that either."

Haywood complimented Wright on a profile he had written on the boxer Joe Louis in the Communist publication *New Masses*. He could see that Wright was a powerful, talented writer, but he wanted him to give up that work entirely for now and focus on organizing protests against the rising cost of living.

"Dick," Haywood said, "the party has decided that you are to accept this work."

Wright, faced with accepting the assignment or quitting the party, chose the former. He soon found himself tabulating "the daily value of pork chops," when his real, obvious strength was writing. The Communists could not see or didn't care that they were wasting a great talent.

One of Wright's critics in the party was a black United States Army veteran named Oliver Law, described by Jane as "rigid, disciplined, devoted." He, too, wanted Wright to give up writing altogether and to associate only with "guaranteed pure" comrades, which infuriated Wright. "To Law, Dick was a hopelessly muddled, sentimental, possibly cowardly person," Jane said.[11]

As Wright's relationship with the party deteriorated, Jane finally asked Herbert, a man of strong standing and clout in the organization, to have a talk with him. Newton, like many other Communists, was suspicious of the "moral strength and intellectual integrity" of artists, Jane said. However, Newton believed that once American society and its economic structure were "reorganized" by the Communists, artists would have more freedom. First, there had to be a revolution, and Wright was too impatient to wait for that, Herbert said. Wright cared more for his own immediate career success than for the larger, long-term goal of improving life for Americans blacks, Herbert believed.

"So Newton was not an artist," Jane said. "Dick wanted

to have things easier right then. Impasse."[12]

The unanswered question was exactly how long Wright and other Communist artists would have to wait until a revolution transformed society to the point that the luxury of art could be indulged. Herbert Newton seemed to believe that the revolution was imminent, that the endless strikes, protests, and bloody street clashes with police were somehow going to amount to something. But what if they didn't? What if Americans in general, or African Americans specifically, never took to Communism? What then? Would there be nothing left but the endless infighting, labels, and paranoia that seemed to dominate the American Communist Party? Few seemed to be asking these questions except for Wright, who in retrospect was wise for looking after his own career first.

Wright was not a man who could be told what to think, what to read, and especially what to write, and the Communist Party was clearly not a place that would allow him to flourish. He was not at all happy that his own race seemed to be kicking him out of the revolution, that he was a man apart from his race who was in fact ridiculed for his pretensions of grandeur.

As Wright was drifting away from the party, the Newtons grew ever closer to it. In 1936, the party offered an all-expense-paid trip to Moscow not only for Herbert but for Jane and their two children. It would be a time for study and renewal.

Newton was reaching the position of a senior figure in the American Communist movement, even though he was only thirty-two years old. It had been nearly a decade since he traveled to the Soviet Union for study, and he had made a name for himself as a serious, on-the-street agitator who could spark headlines for the party both in the Deep South, where he still faced a death sentence, and in Chicago, where his wife was put on trial for her sanity.

Newton was now traveling in international Communist circles as a member of the Profintern, which in 1930 had named a special International Negro Committee to focus on producing "strikes and revolts" among blacks throughout the world, including South Africa, Rhodesia, and the United States.[13]

In the spring of 1936, as Newton was headed back to Moscow, Victor Ridder, the head of the New Deal's Works Progress Administration, released an internal agency report warning that an organization of WPA workers called the City Projects Council was controlled by Communists and was linked to the Trade Union Unity League, the American division of the Profintern.[14]

Communists were clearly involved in many New Deal programs, including the Federal Negro Theater and the Federal Writers' Project, where Richard Wright found himself working in Chicago as he moved from one relief job to the next. Wright's Communist coworkers gave him the silent treatment. He was considered a traitor after his falling out with the party. "I sat beside them in the office, ate next to them in restaurants, and rode up and down in the elevators with them but they all looked straight ahead, wordlessly," Wright remembered.[15]

In Moscow, Herbert Newton was no longer using the revolutionary name Gilmer Brady but rather Tom Sawyer, which did not exactly fit the tough-guy image of a veteran street fighter and agitator. In documents, Newton described himself as a journalist, a job title he always used alternately with agitprop director.[16]

Back home in the United States, the harassment would not stop. In May 1936, more than a year after the eviction fight, the Illinois Emergency Relief Commission obtained a criminal warrant charging Jane with fraud.[17] The commission claimed that in December 1934, the same month as the eviction, Jane had represented herself as Harriet Williams, the landlord, and received an eighteen-dollar check for rent of the apartment "occupied by Herbert and Jane Newton." Jane then signed her own name and the landlord's name to the check and cashed it, the warrant said.

When police went to arrest Jane, she wasn't there. She had already left for the Soviet Union to join Herbert. Jane had told neighbors that "she expected to stay in Russia because there her marriage to a colored man would be approved," said G. B. Foley, attorney for the relief commission.

Reporters called Jane's father, John Emery, in Grand Rapids for comment. He didn't even know his daughter had left for Russia, describing their relationship as "estranged." Jane had been a brilliant student, John Emery said. "However, I believe communism and other isms have unbalanced her mind. Perhaps when she lives in the Soviet, she will finally wake up to her delusion."

She didn't.

Jane enjoyed the trip. The Communists "wined and dined" her and Herbert, the third of the Newtons' five children, Dolores, later said. There was free day care for the children. When Jane walked in one afternoon to pick them up, she heard her daughter Michelle speaking Russian.[18] There was even a side trip to Paris for both Jane and Herbert for a meeting on Profintern business.[19]

Jane may have been enamored of her vacation in Russia, but for many of those who lived there permanently, the country was no picnic. One of those was Robert Robinson, the African American recruited to the Soviet Union while a worker at Ford Motor Company in 1930. By 1936, he was a Soviet citizen enduring Stalin's "Great Purge," in which the Communist dictator imprisoned or executed his perceived political opponents. Robinson had escaped American racism only to find a universe that in many ways was more terrifying.

At the machine shop where Robinson worked, more than twenty workers "suddenly disappeared" between 1934 and 1936, never to be seen or heard from again.

Fear of saying the wrong thing to a person who could turn out to be a government informant was paralyzing. "Informers were in practically every housing development, but it was difficult to tell who they were," Robinson wrote. "It could be a kindly-appearing old lady or it could be your best friend. The terror was such that no one dared to speak, even to a relative on the street, without looking over his shoulder first and then only in a whisper."[20]

One couple told Robinson that if they ever heard a knock on their door after eleven-thirty at night, they would hug and kiss each other and their children goodbye before opening the door, so likely was it that the caller was the secret police coming to take them away forever.

Among those killed in Stalin's purges was Lovett Fort-Whiteman, the Texan who had been one of the earliest African American converts to the Communist Party and a recruiter for the school Newton attended, KUTV. In the winter of 1938–39, he starved to death in a forced labor camp where he had been sent for criticizing the Soviet government.

He had been severely beaten in the camp, all of his teeth knocked out.

Many on the American left were falling out of love with Stalin. Yet Earl Browder, head of the American Communist Party, defended the purges, comparing the victims to the American general Benedict Arnold or the secessionists in the American South.[21] What choice did Browder have but to defend Stalin, unless he was willing to quit the party and his career? In a later debate, a Socialist pointed out that it was but an accident of geography that Browder, living safely in the United States, was not himself a victim of Stalin's purges.[22]

Stalin's Great Purge took a toll on KUTV. More than half of the faculty and administrative staff there "disappeared," to the point that the school was finally closed in 1938.[23]

Herbert Newton's government file in the Russian archives ends with the 1936 trip to Moscow with Jane and the kids. The Soviet government clearly lost interest in the American black revolution. The new focus was fascism, particularly in Germany and Italy, which posed a major threat to Communism and the Soviet Union.

In 1936, Spain appeared to be the next domino after leftists won the 1936 elections, but General Francisco Franco staged a revolt against the new government, sparking a civil war. Germany and Italy both sent aid to Franco, while Communists from all over the world sent volunteers to support Spain's Popular Front government, which included Socialists and Communists. American Communists sent volunteers, including Milton Herndon, Angelo's brother, and Oliver Law, both of whom would die in the fighting.

Harry Haywood, head of the American Communist

Party's "Negro Department," the man so despised by Richard Wright, spent six months in Spain during the war, the highest-ranking American Communist to do so.

Haywood entered Spain through France and immediately began suffering from asthma attacks, struggling to keep up with the march through mountainous terrain.

In combat, he could not seem to get along with his fellow soldiers. The same type of political infighting that was common within the ranks of the American Communist Party surfaced on the battlefield in Spain. It often seemed impossible for Communists to get along, which distracted them from the larger goals they were trying to achieve.

With food and water running short during combat, Haywood volunteered to leave the front line and retrieve supplies. He thought his commanding officer, Jock Cunningham, understood that. As a political commissar, Haywood believed his primary duty was to keep up morale among the soldiers, and there was no better way to do that than with food and water.

But when Haywood returned with supplies, Cunningham screamed at him, "Where in the hell have you been?"[24]

"Rounding up the kitchens, you knew that," Haywood replied.

"Fuck the kitchens, you should have been here," the commander said.

When Haywood returned to the United States, he immediately learned of the intra-party rumor against him—that he had abandoned his battlefield post without permission, that he had run away. His career would never recover. This was the man who was supposed to be leading American blacks into Communist revolution.

In late 1936, Benjamin Mays, who was then head of the Howard University School of Religion and who would soon be president of Morehouse College in Atlanta, found himself in India on a trip sponsored by the YMCA.

The headmaster of an Indian school for "untouchables" specifically asked to meet Mays, who was one of thirteen black American delegates on the trip. At the school, Mays had dinner with the students. After the meal, the headmaster introduced Mays as an American "untouchable" who had suffered under his country's system of segregation but had overcome that discrimination.[25]

"I was proof that they, too, could be 'somebody worthwhile,' " Mays remembered.

Mays, a Baptist minister, had never thought of himself or American blacks as "untouchables," but he suddenly realized it was an accurate comparison. "In my country, I was segregated almost everywhere I went, always in the South and often in the North," he wrote. "I was not permitted to eat or sleep in white hotels or restaurants and was barred from worship in white churches."

Mays predicted that untouchability would be outlawed in India before segregation was outlawed in the United States. He was correct.

While in India, Mays managed to arrange a meeting with Mahatma Gandhi, leader of the nonviolent movement for Indian rights and independence from British rule. When Mays told Gandhi that he had canceled a tour of the Taj Mahal in order to meet the leader, Gandhi replied, "You chose wisely. When you come to India again, the Taj Mahal will be there. I may not be here."[26]

Nonviolent protest, Gandhi explained in their ninety-minute conversation, was exercised out of strength, not weakness. "Nonviolence must never be practiced as a technique or strategy because one is too weak to use violence," Mays remembered Gandhi telling him. "It must be practiced in absolute love and without hate. One may have to call off a nonviolent campaign if hate develops and love ceases to be the dominant motivation for action."

Mays asked Gandhi about the charge that a nonviolent protester who violated the law had no respect for it. "Gandhi's response was that the nonviolent man is law-abiding in that he is willing to pay the price when he disobeys unjust laws," he recalled.

The fight for African American equality in the United States was slowly evolving on both conflicting and parallel tracks. There was the Communist movement, which advocated immediate overthrow—through violence, if necessary—of the United States government and the nation's economic system, to be replaced by a Soviet-style regime. Then there were Christian ministers such as Mays, who were inspired by nonviolence and Gandhi but seemed to their critics to be moving at glacial speed. Aligned with the Christian ministers was the mainstream NAACP, which focused on the courts for justice and was also criticized for moving too slowly.

It was clear that change was in the air, that the American system of racial discrimination was not sustainable in the long term. There was going to be a revolution.

Who would lead it? Would it happen soon or decades later? Would it be violent or nonviolent?

Those were the unanswered questions.

CHAPTER 8

A Native
SON

In August 1936, the Newton family traveled back from Moscow to the United States, but not to Chicago, where there was a warrant out for Jane's arrest for allegedly illegally cashing an eighteen-dollar relief check. The Newtons went instead to New York, where Herbert, whose nickname among close friends was "Cully," was stationed at American party headquarters.

Just as the Soviets were losing interest in the American Communist Party, so, too, was the United States electorate. In the 1936 elections, the Communists put up Earl Browder for president and James Ford for vice president. In another landslide for FDR, the Communists received only 80,159 votes, 20,000 fewer than they had four years earlier. Roosevelt received a staggering 27.4 million votes. A year earlier, FDR had achieved perhaps his most lasting program, Social Security, which promised retirement checks for millions. It did not officially kick off until 1940, but in the meantime, Congress offered block grants to states if they would administer their own "old-age pensions."

In Georgia, Governor Eugene Talmadge, a racist who was open about his views and benefited from them politically, wouldn't take the federal government grants. In a telling remark about the relationship between racism and capitalism in the Deep South, Talmadge flatly stated that Social Security would encourage blacks to stop working, cutting off Georgia's supply of cheap labor. Talmadge had been just as honest in 1934 when Angelo Herndon was about to be released on bond. The writer Theodore Dreiser had called the governor personally to make sure that Herndon would be able to get out of the state safely, since there had been threats that he would be lynched. "We never molest a nigger unless he rapes a white woman," Talmadge told Dreiser.[1]

In New York, just as in Chicago, the Newtons had to worry about finding a place to live, walking a fine line, even in the North, as an interracial couple. "We had to live in the ghetto because of his color," Jane wrote. "We had a system, Cully and I, in which he found the house and I moved us. If I had appeared while he was arranging the house, we would have been refused."[2]

By the spring of 1937, the Newtons were living in a rented brownstone at 175 Carleton Avenue in Brooklyn. Just as they were settling into their new home, the United States Supreme Court, in a vote of five to four, overturned Angelo Herndon's conviction and ruled Georgia's insurrection law unconstitutional. This was the same law Herbert Newton and the other members of the Atlanta Six had been charged with breaking, so their legal troubles were over as well.

The Georgia statute used to arrest Herndon, Newton, and the other defendants was so vague as to be nothing more than "a dragnet which may enmesh any one who agitates for a change of government," the Supreme Court ruled. The Georgia law violated both freedom of speech and freedom of assembly, the court said.[3]

But Justice Willis Van Devanter dissented, arguing that the Communists were hardly advocating a change of government through peaceful means such as the ballot box. He cited a donation receipt book found in Herndon's possession that stated, "Every dollar collected is a bullet fired into the boss class." And the idea of forming a separate black nation, of seizing the land owned by white farmers, could be achieved only with "force and violence," the justice wrote.

At the time of the Supreme Court ruling, Herndon, like Newton, was working for the party out of New York, as was Herndon's trial attorney, Benjamin Davis Jr., who in 1936 joined the staff of the *Daily Worker*.

For the Communists, the Herndon ruling was a huge legal victory. They had changed American law. Georgia would not be able to use the old insurrection law ever again against anyone. Yet in the end, it was really the American legal system and the Constitution—neither of which the Communists respected—that had saved the day.

This had been clear in the Scottsboro case. The Communists had eventually lost control of it after International Labor Defense attempted to bribe one of the alleged rape victims, Victoria Price, in exchange for changing her testimony. This prompted the chief defense attorney, Samuel Leibowitz, to announce that he would quit unless all Communists were removed from the case.

Benjamin Davis had tried to salvage the case for the Communists, traveling to Alabama and telling the Scottsboro defendants that the bribery charges were faked by the "Alabama lynchers," but it was too late.[4] The case was turned over to a coalition of black ministers, whom the *Daily Worker* called "bootlicking Harlem preachers." Leibowitz stayed on as defense counsel.

Shortly after the Supreme Court cleared Angelo Herndon and, by extension, Herbert Newton, Richard Wright, his career as a writer gaining traction, also migrated to New York, escaping the Chicago Communists, many of whom he had thoroughly alienated. He also hoped to make connections with the big publishers.[5]

Wright lived briefly with the Newtons in Brooklyn before finding a room in Harlem. Starting with a clean slate with the New York Communists, Wright landed a job in the Harlem bureau of the *Daily Worker*. The bureau chief was Ben Davis Jr.

Wright cranked out stories for the *Daily Worker* but privately grumbled about having to write "propaganda" for "Stalin's newspaper." The New York Communists eventually also grew suspicious of Wright as an intellectual. In many ways, he was back where he had been in Chicago. "It was not for this that I came to NYC," Wright told his new friend and future best-selling author Ralph Ellison.[6]

But in late 1937, Wright's career began to surge when he won a national short-story contest. The prize was five hundred dollars and, better yet, publication by Harper Brothers of his book of short stories, entitled *Uncle Tom's Children*.

Wright was then living in a rooming house in Harlem on 143rd Street. He developed a serious relationship with the landlady's daughter, a black woman named Marion Sawyer. In May 1938, they announced wedding plans.

The woman's mother was impressed with Wright not because he was an up-and-coming writer but because he was "quiet, did not get drunk or start trouble and dressed neatly," Jane remembered. In fact, the landlady and her daughter were baffled that Wright could make a living at all as a writer.[7] "They were a little puzzled as to how he could be living without some racket, even said some things that indicated they believed he might be but were content with his story inasmuch as he paid his rent regularly," Jane recalled.

Then the wedding was abruptly canceled when Marion failed the blood test for their marriage license. She tested positive for congenital syphilis, transmitted from her mother at birth.

"He handed the notice to me to read without saying much," Jane remembered. "Just something about it's being a stunning piece of news. I urged him to see that she got treatment immediately and realized this was unlikely for he could think of nothing but getting out of that rooming house as soon as possible."

Jane had sensed that Wright never loved Marion but was shocked by his "complete and total withdrawal" from her following the diagnosis. According to one of Wright's biographers, Hazel Rowley, Wright would regret his cruelty to Marion for the rest of his life.

A few days after the blood-test results, Wright moved in with the Newtons at 175 Carleton Avenue. The Newtons, who now had a third child, Dolores, made room for him in the back parlor overlooking the garden. He was working on a new novel, *Native Son*, which would go on to become one of the most important works of fiction ever written on race in America.

Wright told Jane that black people always knew what white people were thinking, a skill they had acquired from years of slavery and servitude. But the reverse, he said, was never true.

In *Native Son*, Wright did not seek pity from white readers. Instead, he wanted to show them the results of their racism, the effects of creating a permanent, alienated black underclass in America. It had likely never occurred to many white people that racism, stretched out over centuries in the North and the South, would take a toll on those who were on the receiving end. Wright wanted oblivious whites to see this. He wanted to "condemn them entirely to the contemplation of their image in his mirror," Jane said.[8]

Native Son is the story of a young, restless black man on the South Side of Chicago, Bigger Thomas. The Great Depression is on, and Bigger and his neighborhood friends are making ends meet by robbing black merchants only, because police tended not to investigate those crimes thoroughly. They were much more likely to get caught if they robbed a white man.

Bigger feels boxed in by the segregated society of the South Side in the 1930s. He glances up at an airplane in the sky and wonders why black people are not allowed to be pilots. A friend advises Bigger to get used to it, but he can't let it go, comparing life under segregation to living in jail.[9]

It was Wright's way of describing the torture of segregation. Blacks were bombarded by the glitter of white society but could not partake of it. It was cruel in the South, yes, but in some ways it was even more difficult to take in a bustling city such as Chicago, with all its dazzling lights, buildings, movies, newspapers, and radios that taunted blacks, made them want what they could not have.

"Sometimes, in areas far removed from Mississippi, I'd hear a Negro say, 'I wish I didn't have to live this way, I feel like I want to burst.' " Wright said. "But then the anger would pass, he would go back to his job and try to eke out a few pennies to support his wife and children."

Blacks found solace and escape in religion, believing that "the more bitter life was in the present, the happier it would be in the hereafter."[10] Others wished for their own country, their own flag, so they could have a place they could own and control, Wright said.

He based Bigger Thomas on all the black men he had known over the years who defied Jim Crow. Most of them ended up dead or in prison. Wright was also influenced by his work at the Boys Club on the South Side of Chicago, which was filled with hundreds of Bigger Thomases.

"Here I felt for the first time that the rich white folk who were paying my salary did not really give a goddamn about Bigger, that their kindness was prompted at bottom by a selfish motive," Wright said. "They were paying me to distract Bigger with ping pong, checkers, swimming, marbles, and baseball in order that he might not roam the streets and harm the valuable white property. I am not condemning Boy's [sic] Clubs and ping pong as such; but these little stopgaps were utterly inadequate to fill up the centuries-long chasm of emptiness which American civilization had created in these Biggers."[11]

In *Native Son*, Wright explored the obsession with keeping black men away from white women, while at the same time movies and advertisements were filled with sultry, sexualized images of them. A black man who defied convention and dated a white woman could find himself charged with rape and be imprisoned or lynched. A white woman such as Jane might find herself in a sanity trial.

The first chapter of *Native Son* includes two contrasting scenes: the cramped, rat-infested apartment where Bigger lives and a movie newsreel of Mary Dalton, the daughter of a wealthy white Chicago real-estate mogul, frolicking on the beach in Florida with a Communist friend. Wright named the character Mary Dalton after Mary Licht, the white Communist who was arrested in Atlanta with Herbert Newton in 1930, along with the other members of the Atlanta Six. The party later transferred her to Chicago.

"Dick didn't know her very well but rather disliked her on principle and felt very mischievous using her name," Jane recalled. "He knew Harry Haywood and the other Chicago Communists would recognize the name and would be properly taken aback by it," Jane said.[12]

Mary Dalton is actually a lot like Jane: a young, beautiful woman, daughter of a wealthy real-estate man, who defies her family and embraces Communism. In the novel, Mary meets Bigger Thomas when he lands a relief job as the family's chauffeur. When Bigger shows up for work, he immediately becomes a different person, transforming from a brash young street thug to a subdued servant. In the Dalton household, Bigger uses expressions such as "yessuh" and "nawsuh." He is conscious of every word he says, every action he takes, even the direction of his eyes, lest he be accused of staring at the women of the household. This is not the way Bigger normally talks or acts. It is the way he is forced to behave in the presence of white people, a maddening change of persona, described by Benjamin Mays and others, that is demanded by the racial customs of the day.

As Wright toiled away on *Native Son*, Jane was right there at 175 Carleton Avenue, busily raising her three children. Herbert would rise at the crack of dawn to read and study, then was off to his Communist Party job at nine, often returning late in the evening. Wright would usually be up as soon as "the sun had warmed the air a little." He would take a yellow pad, a fountain pen, and a bottle of ink and write on a bench at nearby Fort Green Park, returning at ten for breakfast.

As in most households with young children, it was often a chaotic scene at the Newtons'. "By ten, when Dick came down from the park, the children would be playing in the backyard and I would be clearing the decks for the next meal," Jane wrote. "We ate in the kitchen, which was large and light and it was the center of all kinds of activities going on in a family of children; washing, ironing, playing, sewing, fighting, bathing."[13]

Wright was not good with the Newton children. "He teased and frightened them and they were never fond of him," Jane said.

Somehow, Jane and Wright found time to discuss *Native Son*, "although sometimes we had to rather shout our opinions across something resembling a bear pit," Jane said. Still, Wright sought Jane's input as he wrote, and she helped shape the novel.

On his first day on the job, Bigger Thomas is instructed

to drive Mary Dalton to a university lecture downtown, but she directs him instead to take her to a rendezvous with her white Communist boyfriend, Jan.

Although Bigger is about the same age as Mary and Jan, he still feels forced to use servile lingo. But Jan immediately breaks the protocol, shaking Bigger's hand and refusing to let go. "Don't say *sir* to me," says Jan. "I'll call you Bigger and you'll call me Jan."[14]

This is the instant racial equality the Communists were promoting, but for Bigger it is confusing, frustrating, and awkward because it does not exist anywhere outside their isolated, idealistic world. In the real world, Bigger is still a black man, still a chauffeur.

Jan takes over the driving, and Mary also sits in the front seat. Here are the three of them—a white man, a white woman, and a black man, Bigger—all sitting side by side, all seemingly equal, but not really, not at all. If only it were that easy.

Driving along the shore of Lake Michigan, Jan points out the tall buildings and tells Bigger, "We'll own all that some day, Bigger. After the revolution it'll all be ours. But we'll have to fight for it. . . . And when that day comes, things'll be different. There'll be no white or no black; there'll be no rich and no poor."[15]

Bigger can't help feeling that Jan and the Communists are using him for their revolution, patronizing him: "He felt that this white man, having helped put him down, having helped deform him, held him up now to look at him, and be amused. At the moment he felt toward Mary and Jan a dumb, cold and inarticulate hate."[16]

It gets worse when Jan demands that Bigger take them

to "one of those places where colored people eat." They force Bigger to go inside with them, to eat with them as equals. This is embarrassing to Bigger because he is a regular at the restaurant and the Communists are asking him to act as if they have traveled through time to a new day when everyone is equal, black and white. Then Jan buys a bottle of rum, and he and Mary insist that Bigger drink with them. So they are all sloppy drunk, in a pretend world of racial equality.

On the drive home comes more patronizing, more stereotyping. Jan and Mary, sitting in the backseat now, discuss black people and the Communist movement.

"They have so much *emo*tion!" Mary says. "What a people! If we could ever get them going . . ."

"We can't have a revolution without 'em," Jan replies. "They've got to be organized. They've got spirit. They'll give the Party something it needs."[17]

"And their songs—the spirituals! Aren't they marvelous?" Mary says. "Say, Bigger, can you sing?" She then belts out a rendition of "Swing Low, Sweet Chariot."

Jan and Mary are oblivious to the dangerous situation they have inflicted on Bigger, who is responsible for making sure Mary arrives safely at home. Even more dangerous is the fact that Jan and Mary have sex in the backseat as Bigger drives them.

After dropping Jan off, Bigger arrives at the Dalton household and has to carry Mary up the stairs to her room— a black man, himself reeking of rum, carrying a passed-out white woman to her bed. If he is discovered, he will at best lose his new job. At worst, he will be accused of rape. This is the real world, not the fantasyland of the Communist Party. How many ways can a black man be whipsawed?

As Bigger places Mary in the bed, he can't resist the temptation to kiss her and touch her breasts. Then the door creaks. Mary's mother, who is blind, is standing there.

"Mary?" Mrs. Dalton says.

Mary mumbles.

Bigger panics. He holds his hand over Mary's mouth and finally puts a pillow over her face. "He had to stop her from mumbling, or he would be caught," the narrator says.

When Mrs. Dalton leaves the room, Mary is dead. Mrs. Dalton doesn't realize this, but she can smell rum in the room.

Bigger stuffs Mary's body in a trunk and drags it to the basement. There, he sees the blazing coal furnace and tries to put Mary's body in it, but it won't fit. So he chops her head off with a hatchet.

It was over this scene that Jane and Wright had one of their most vigorous literary discussions. Wright had Bigger using an ordinary pocketknife to behead Mary. Jane insisted that was unrealistic. To prove her point, she went to the grocery store and purchased a hen. She sharpened an ordinary kitchen knife with a blade about the same size as a pocketknife and handed it to Wright. He tried to cut the chicken's neck as it drooped over the table but found he couldn't. Jane was correct.[18]

In *Native Son*, Bigger tries to sever Mary's head with his pocketknife and fails, then turns to a hatchet he spots in the basement. Bigger also ends up killing his girlfriend, Bessie. He is turning out to be a true monster.

Jane thought it unnecessary to kill Bessie. Wright had already established the evil of Bigger's character and the society that had produced him, Jane argued. But Wright insisted.

At that time, he still had no ending for *Native Son* but be-lieved that "every so often, something very exciting, disturb-ing, violent must happen" to keep the reader's interest. As they were debating whether or not Bessie should be killed, there was a knock on the door. It was Jane's landlord, "star-ing uneasily at us" with thoughts that they were planning a real murder.

Wright had continual discussions with Jane but would go for weeks without seeing Herbert, who, committed revolutionary that he was, often returned home late, af-ter everyone had turned in for the night. Once, Jane men-tioned to Wright something that Herbert had said to her, and Wright asked, "When does Cully ever talk to you?"[19] Wright didn't understand that Jane would sleep in the evenings, then wake up to see Herbert when he arrived home, often after midnight. "Somehow [Wright] didn't realize that we went to bed together each night, breakfasted every morning with our children, and that my husband came home each night to dinner—late but home."

When Jane and Herbert moved to a new house or apart-ment—dancing the dance as always with landlords who might not want to rent to an interracial family—Wright moved with them. For more than a year, Wright and the Newtons were a family unit. Wright even felt comfortable enough to complain about the way Jane made cornbread. He called her recipe "white folks' style." Wright liked his corn-bread soggy, with less eggs and meal, which Jane realized was an economic issue more than anything. "If one can af-ford eggs and baking powder, the bread is lighter but if one has to do with sour milk, little wheat flour and an inefficient oven, what results is the kind Dick made," Jane wrote.[20]

While they were living at 555 Gates Avenue in Brooklyn, Ralph Ellison began visiting Wright more frequently, their friendship growing. Later, the Newtons and Wright moved to 101 Lefferts Place in Brooklyn, and playwright Ted Ward took an apartment in the same building. Jane had just finished reading the Spanish Civil War novel *Man's Hope* by André Malraux and was rereading Tolstoy's *War and Peace*.

Meanwhile, the story of Bigger Thomas was coming to a close. Arrested for the two murders and surely headed to the electric chair, Bigger actually feels empowered. While other blacks might have endured by losing themselves in religion or liquor, Bigger has struck back at the suffocating system of segregation, "the crime of being black."

Wright earnestly believed that black men in particular were saddled from birth with the curse of blackness. "That little black devil," Wright's own grandmother, who was white, once called him.

"The black man grew in time to hate in himself that which other people hated in him," Wright told a white psychiatrist, Fredric Wertham, who would later open a clinic in Harlem for black teenagers. American racism as described by Wright was a complex organism of fear, sex, religion, economics, and white blindness to the harm it inflicted.[21]

In *Native Son*, Wright depicted two parallel and competing forces that were then trying to shape the future of the nine million African Americans. After Bigger is captured, Jan, the white Communist, and a local black preacher are in the same room with Bigger at the jail. Wright didn't have much hope, then or later, that either group would succeed.

At the Lefferts Place apartment, a typist hired by Wright appeared each day to prepare the final manuscript for submission to the publisher.

"When the typing was done, we joyfully read the entire manuscript from beginning to end, one after the other of us, Ted [Ward], my friend Elaine Mason (she's a painter and at that time lived just a few blocks away), and a couple of other people," Jane wrote. "The house was always full of people, coming and going, upstairs and downstairs."[22]

Jane had a record of Shostakovich's Prelude in E-flat Minor. "We put it on Dick's phonograph and turned it as loud as we could and played it at the end of a fine night of drinking and celebrating," Jane remembered. "The walls shook, even in that pretty solid old house."

CHAPTER 9

DECIMATION

Shortly after Wright submitted his typed manuscript of *Native Son* to the publisher in the spring of 1939, the Newtons' age-old landlord problem resurfaced. This time, the landlord was black, a West Indian, and he, too, objected to the mixing of the races under his roof.

"Dick talked to him, my husband talked to him but he was adamant," said Jane. "It seems that the West Indians, in Brooklyn anyhow, were thought to be much more conservative, even reactionary, than native American Negroes."[1]

Wright responded by loudly playing Jamaican songs including "Sly Mongoose" on his phonograph. Then it was time to start house hunting again.

That same spring, Herbert Newton invited a young white woman and fellow Communist, Ellen Poplowitz, home to Lefferts Place for coffee after a party executive meeting. Jane described Ellen, who was then twenty-six years old, as "very pretty, a pale very young face, framed in dark curls, quiet and serious." Poplowitz was a leader of the party's Fulton Street branch in Brooklyn, as was Jane. But Jane hardly had time for meetings. She was usually at home nights with her three children.

Herbert introduced Poplowitz to Wright. "My memory of it is that Dick liked her at once and they became friendly very quickly," Jane wrote.[2]

With the June 1 deadline approaching to vacate Lefferts Place, Wright, preparing for the launch of *Native Son*, decided to go his own way this time, following Ted Ward to Harlem.

That summer, however, Wright visited the Newtons, who were now living in yet another Brooklyn brownstone, and he brought Ellen with him. Wright wanted Jane to talk to Ellen about life as an interracial couple, a topic on which Jane was now an expert.

"She wanted to marry him and he was very much attached to her," Jane wrote. "But she couldn't make up her mind to do it because of her family. She told me she had refused him but kept wanting to reconsider and felt bad about it."

Jane didn't feel comfortable advising Ellen on what to do. It was a tough, individual decision with huge consequences in a society that openly despised racial mixing. It was not just surly landlords or family estrangement that Jane had been forced to endure as a result of her choice to marry Herbert. She had also been placed in a mental hospital.

"I could tell her that inter-marriage isn't easy to live with, that not only families are unfriendly," Jane wrote. "One can't really say to a girl what to do."[3]

In August 1939, as Jane and the kids were packing up

for a trip to Martha's Vineyard to escape the summer heat of Brooklyn, Wright mentioned that he had met another woman, a divorced dancer of Russian-Jewish ancestry named Dhimah Meidman. They married on August 12 at a church in Harlem. Ralph Ellison and his wife, Rose, witnessed the wedding.

Native Son, published in the spring of 1940, was an instant bestseller and a Book of the Month Club selection, selling 215,000 copies in its first three weeks.[4] Wright was newly famous and soon to be wealthy at the ripe young age of thirty-two.

Sterling North, a white literary editor in Chicago, called it "one of the strongest and more fearless novels I have ever read—359 pages of black dynamite. I only hope it doesn't start race riots in Chicago as it easily might if not handled with circumspection."[5]

During a public talk on the book in Iowa, two women approached a reviewer, Edith Webber, and rebuked her for even discussing it, "the idea being the book stirs up negro-hatred. . . . It 'puts ideas' into the negroes' minds."[6] The critics were missing the premise of the novel, Webber wrote, which was that "we make" men like Bigger Thomas.

Wright flatly predicted violence unless white society came to grips with the permanent black underclass it perpetuated in the Bigger Thomases of the world. "He lives amid the greatest possible plenty on earth and he is looking and feeling for a way out," said Wright. "Bigger Thomas, conditioned as his organism is, will not become an ardent or even lukewarm supporter of the status quo."[7]

In a "vague sense," Bigger was a black nationalist, Wright went on to explain, because he was "a native son but he was not allowed to live as an American."

Predictably, many in the American Communist Party did not like *Native Son*, including Ben Davis Jr., Angelo Herndon's lawyer, who in a review for the *Daily Worker* criticized Wright for his broad-brush portrayal of young blacks as desperate killers. "The average unemployed Negro youth does not become a rapist and a murderer," Davis wrote."[8]

However, in a personal letter to Wright, Davis said he had learned much from reading *Native Son* and felt "enriched" by the novel.[9]

Agreeing with Davis's criticism of the novel was none other than Herbert Newton, who in a letter to Davis congratulated him on his "swell job" with the *Native Son* review.[10]

Wright pointed out to his Communist critics that Bigger was not meant to portray all blacks but was an extreme symbol of oppression, of what happened when an oppressed people were pushed too far and simply couldn't take it anymore. "I made Mrs. Dalton blind to symbolize how millions today do not realize or admit this," Wright wrote Mike Gold, a writer at the *Daily Worker*.[11]

But the truth was that if the Communist Party could have had its way, *Native Son* would never have been written. Wright would likely have been focused not on fiction but on the price of pork chops.

Playwright Ted Ward warned Wright, who was by now only a marginal member of the Communist Party, that his comrades were fuming over *Native Son*. "They were all for setting up a bureau to which writers like you would have to submit their materials before publishing them," Ward wrote. "The idea was really stupid but you would be surprised to know how heated they became when I opposed it. Another thing was that you should be forced to attend meetings and do party work so that you would learn how not to make such a mistake as *Native Son*."[12]

Wright absolutely despised Communist Party censorship. As he was working on *Native Son* in New York, Margaret Walker, a fellow writer and Communist in Chicago, had written to tell him that a woman named Hortense Barr had been named head of the local party's "writers' unit." Wright did not dislike Barr personally but felt she had no business supervising writers. "I dropped your letter like a hot potato and simply said to myself, that goddamned, sonofabitching, motherfucking bastard party leadership in Chicago," Wright replied to Walker.[13] He urged her to "fight for your rights or get out. Don't let them boobs hamstring you."

Wright rejected any type of censorship, even from himself. He worried that he would pull punches, not wanting to offend the Communists or middle-income blacks with the unredeeming character of Bigger Thomas, and also not wanting to give white readers material they could use to say, "See, didn't we tell you all along that niggers are like that?"

The larger issue transcended politics and even race, Wright believed. It was the human right of every person to "think and feel honestly" that was sadly absent in the Communist world but was a necessary ingredient to produce a powerful, epic novel such as *Native Son*.

Wright told Jane he wanted to hold a mirror up to white society, to show it the effects of its racism. And hundreds of thousands of white readers were buying *Native Son*, despite its ominous message of black violence against whites.

Was *Native Son*'s success a sign that whites were open to change?

"Perhaps the country is a little more civilized than we thought," Wright's editor, Edward Aswell, wrote him on June 12, 1940, as the book continued to sell well. The world situation was imploding, Paris having fallen just a week earlier to the Nazis. Amid this depressing news, Aswell saw a bright spot in the American reaction to *Native Son*, written by a black Communist from Mississippi.

"I venture to say that if your book had been written 10 or 15 years ago that it would not have had anything like the reception that it has had," Aswell wrote. "In spite of much evidence to the contrary, times do change."[14]

In Hollywood, however, *Native Son* was too hot to handle. Only a year after the release of the blockbuster movie that glorified the Confederacy, *Gone With the Wind*, the studios wouldn't touch it. William James Fadiman of Metro-Goldwyn-Mayer Pictures felt compelled to contact Wright's agent, Paul Reynolds Jr., with praise of *Native Son* as a "sociological document of great power" but added that it was "obviously outlawed for the screen by its subject matter."[15]

Amid the excitement and controversy over the release of *Native Son*, the Newtons saw little of Wright. "His public life claimed him," said Jane.

Wright decided to take a trip to Mexico on a belated honeymoon with his new wife, Dhimah, but it did not go well. When he returned to New York in the summer of 1940, he was back at the Newton household in Brooklyn, alone, the marriage to Dhimah finished.

Wright renewed his relationship with Ellen Poplowitz. They lived together at the Newtons' for a few weeks before moving to Harlem and marrying on March 12, 1941, with Benjamin Davis as one of the witnesses. Davis, despite his criticism of *Native Son*, was trying to keep Wright in the Communist fold. At the same time, he borrowed money from Wright, the salary of a career Communist not being comparable to that of a best-selling author. "I am always hard pressed and live week-to-week," the Harvard-educated Davis wrote Wright, a man with only an eight-grade education, in late 1941.[16]

Ellen's marriage to Wright, like Jane's to Herbert Newton, strained her relationship with her parents. Several times, Ellen's mother appeared at the Newtons' apartment, trying to "talk some sense" into her daughter, even pleading with Jane for help, to no avail.[17] The marriage of Ellen and Wright would be controversial, but it would last until his death more than two decades later.

As Wright's career soared, Herbert Newton's job as a revolutionary foot soldier was beginning to take a physical toll.

On July 18, 1941, Newton led a demonstration of the WPA Teachers Union outside New York City mayor Fiorello La Guardia's home on Fifth Avenue. The teachers were protesting layoffs as the WPA and other New Deal programs were winding to a close as war approached and the Depression waned. Newton, listed as vice president of the union, was one of twenty-eight demonstrators arrested after blocking Fifth Avenue.[18]

A police officer named Emmett Howe said that as officers were attempting to break up the demonstration, Newton punched him in the face, breaking his glasses. In a police car on the way to the precinct on East 104th Street, Newton continued to attack the officers, Howe said. Dragging Newton from the car at the police station, the officers found a black-handled razor on the seat of the car, Howe testified in court.

Newton denied ever striking Howe and said he never saw the razor until Howe waved it in the courtroom. Furthermore, he said he was surrounded by police officers at the precinct and was so badly beaten he had to be hospitalized.

"I was punched in the face and kicked," Newton said. "They hit me on the jaw and I fell over a chair. I was taken into a small room and hit on the back of the head. They jumped up and down on my back while I lay on the floor."[19]

Activists in Harlem demanded a public hearing on police brutality following the Newton beating. But when forty witnesses including Newton and a representative from the American Civil Liberties Union appeared at police division headquarters on West 123rd Street, deputy inspector George W. Mulholland said he would meet with witnesses only one at a time behind closed doors. The witnesses walked out.[20]

Newton, represented by lawyers from International Labor Defense, was convicted on November 20 of assaulting a police officer, but a judge dismissed the charge of possessing a razor. Newton faced three years in prison.[21] The Newtons now had four children, following the birth of a second son.

With sentencing set for December, the now-famous Richard Wright tried to rally support for Newton. "This case, as you may have heard, is a labor case, not a criminal one," Wright wrote to prominent white psychiatrist Fredric Wertham on December 7, 1941, the day the Japanese bombed Pearl Harbor. "The trouble [Newton] now finds himself in grew out of his activities on behalf of poverty-stricken teachers who live in Harlem. I do not have to call to your attention the plight of the Negro people in Harlem."[22]

Whether or not Wertham intervened is uncertain, but a judge gave Newton a suspended sentence.[23] He would not have to go to prison. But after the police beating, his life seemed to begin a downward spiral.

Jane and Herbert would go on to have five children—three boys and two girls. They were the focus of Jane's life. "The communist cause—the effort, that was secondary," recalled her daughter Dolores, who went on to become an anthropologist.[24]

As a mother, Jane was devoted to her children, but "it was not required of us that we return [that devotion]," said Dolores. Their mother insisted that the children call her Jane. "She didn't believe that there was any particular obligation that was incurred by us from her having given birth to us."

Whereas Jane nurtured her children, the serious, disciplined Herbert was more of a teacher to them. "My father would use us to hand out leaflets," recalled Dolores. "He was more in the role of teaching us about the system, the evils." The lessons were always in generalities, not the specifics of the inner workings of the Communist Party. In fact, Dolores suddenly realized at age eleven that she wasn't quite sure what her father did for a living.

The eldest three Newton children took art and drama classes at the Jefferson School of Social Sciences at 575 Sixth Avenue. Founded in 1944, the school was labeled by its critics as "an adjunct of the communist party." It would close in the Red Scare of the 1950s because of "unwarranted persecution."[25]

Herbert Newton's physical condition continued to deteriorate following the 1941 beating, and so did his marriage. Jane and Herbert divorced in 1946.

"My mother's position on it was that he just suffered too many beatings, that he wasn't the same person," Dolores said. "My take on it would be that it was just a very hard life."[26]

It was indeed a hard life—raising five children, trying to start a revolution, and, in Herbert's case, being subjected to regular police violence.

It was even harder for Jane after the divorce. She found secretarial jobs. At times, she and the five children were on welfare. Her father died in 1947, still estranged from his daughter and no longer a wealthy man, having lost much of his money, as many people did, in the Great Depression. With John Emery no longer in the picture, Jane was able to reunite with her mother, who met her grandchildren once before she died.[27]

Herbert Newton died of a stroke in 1948 at the age of forty-four. Strokes and high blood pressure ran in Herbert's family, but many Communists believed the police beating in the summer of 1941 contributed to his early death.

William L. Patterson, a fellow student with Herbert at KUTV in Moscow in the late 1920s, spoke at the funeral in Harlem, noting that Herbert had devoted more than half his life to the Communist cause.

But in the end, what did Newton or the party have to show for it all—the protests, the beatings, the trips abroad? Very little.

The Communists had backed a few successful court cases, including Scottsboro and that involving Angelo Herndon. But they had not been able to achieve their main goal of a mass uprising, a revolution. And that was before the mass hysteria of the post–World War II Red Scare. After the war, many American Communists would end up kicked out of the party or in prison.

In July 1945, as the war was drawing to a close, Benjamin Davis dusted off the old idea of a separate black nation in the American South. Davis was now a member of the New York City Council, elected as a Communist representing Harlem. Unlike most Communists, Davis had actually been successful at the ballot box. A second Communist was on the city council as well, a white man named Peter Cacchione.

Abandoning the idea of black nationhood was a mistake, Davis said. "I did not detect the errors because I was not sufficiently mature and equipped as a Marxist," he wrote in the Sunday edition of the *Daily Worker*.[28]

But this was no longer the desperate early 1930s, when times were so hard that the idea of a black nation did not sound far-fetched. After World War II, the Soviet Union was a much more menacing rival, controlling Eastern Europe, including half of Germany. Millions of its troops were still in Europe. It had shown its might by decimating Hitler and was now a true superpower. Also, there was the real threat that it would develop nuclear weapons.

A black organization in Harlem, the Association of Trade and Commerce, called Davis's proposal "damnable."[29] But Davis was not necessarily tone-deaf about America's heightened fears over the new international landscape after the war. Rather, this was internal Communist politics at work. Davis was trying to distance himself from Earl Browder, whom Stalin had decided to oust as head of the American Communist Party in 1945, and who would be booted from the party completely the following year.

By resurrecting the Depression-era idea of black nationhood, Davis might have simply been trying to save his career as a Communist. But his words would come back to haunt him. In 1948, a federal grand jury indicted Davis and ten other American Communist leaders for teaching and advocating "the overthrow and destruction of the United States government by force and violence."[30] It was the Angelo Herndon case all over again. Instead of the state of Georgia, the prosecutor was now the federal government, under the auspices of the 1940 Smith Act. The Communists said the indictments were nothing more than presidential politics. It was an election year, and President Truman was locked in a tight race with Republican Thomas Dewey and was determined to win by hook or crook, said the Communists.

By this time, Richard Wright was watching developments from afar in Paris, where he had moved with his wife and children after the war in the hope of escaping American racism. Even as a best-selling author in New York, he had struggled to buy a home in Greenwich Village, his lawyer telling him no bank would approve a mortgage, for fear that white neighbors would object. In order to buy the three-story brownstone at 13 Charles Street, Wright had been forced to create a shell corporation, the Richelieu Company.[31]

In Paris, Wright was euphoric that for the first time in his life, race was not an issue. "I've seen no racial reactions or racial hate at all," Wright wrote Fredric Wertham in 1946. "The absence of all racial feeling seems a little unreal."[32]

Wright would live in Paris for the rest of his life. He befriended existentialist writers Albert Camus and Jean-Paul Sartre. In fact, *Native Son* and the character of Bigger Thomas exhibited strong existential themes and tendencies. *Native Son* was actually published before Camus's landmark novel, *The Stranger*.

Before he left for Paris, Wright had broken completely from the American Communist Party. In Europe, he watched party developments with interest. "The US Communist Party is a joke over here," Wright told Wertham.[33]

France, however, had a real Communist Party. When Wright estimated that nearly a third of the people favored Communism, he was not far off. In the November 1946 national elections in France, the Communists received 28 percent of the vote.

Two years later, the American Communist Party had declined to the point that it did not even field a candidate for president, instead supporting former vice president Henry Wallace, whose Progressive Party candidacy received only 2.3 percent of the vote, fewer than the States' Rights Democratic Party ticket of South Carolina's segregationist governor, Strom Thurmond.

The American Communist Party was impotent but not necessarily harmless. Decades later, Soviet documents would reveal a direct espionage link between the American Communist Party and the Soviet Union. Earl Browder, whose code name was Helmsman, "handpicked" Soviet intelligence sources, couriers, and group handlers, "except for those involved in atomic espionage," according to the 1999 book *The Haunted Wood*, whose authors were granted rare access to Soviet espionage files.[34]

But espionage was one thing; all nations had spies. Starting a revolution, convincing a country's masses to overthrow a government, was another. That was the much more difficult job of foot soldiers such as Herbert Newton and Benjamin Davis, and they failed.

Even so, Davis, still a city councilman from Harlem, and the other ten American Communists leaders accused by prosecutors of conspiring to overthrow the government stood trial in the federal courthouse in New York's Foley Square in March 1949.

Prosecutors argued that the American party had grown soft during the war years and had become too cooperative with the establishment. That was why the international party had ousted Browder and renewed the decades-old idea of black nationhood.

A government witness and former party member named William O. Nowell, a forty-four-year-old black man then working as a clerk at the United States Immigration and Naturalization Service, described the party's plans for a separate black nation. Nowell had joined a Communist Party cell inside the Ford Motor Company in 1929 and in the early 1930s had enrolled in the Lenin School, which Herbert Newton had also attended. He took classes in "the science of civil war," taught by specialists from the Red Army, Nowell testified.[35]

In Moscow, Nowell was taught that "it was necessary for the communist party of the United States to begin the organization of negroes in the black belt in the South toward the establishment of a separate Negro nation." Black nationhood in the South would get the revolution rolling, sparking the larger goal, which was an uprising of industrial workers in the heavily populated North and throughout the country, said Nowell.

But Nowell dared to disagree with this tactic, openly stating that the Communists were using Southern blacks as fodder. Nationhood would "isolate the Negroes of the South and use them merely as a tool to create a revolution in which these unsuspecting people would be sacrificed for a cause in which they had not the least understanding," said Nowell.

Not surprisingly, Nowell's challenge of the leadership on the "Negro question" had prompted the American Communist Party to bring charges against him at its 1934 convention. Nowell left the party two years later.

Taking the witness stand in his own defense at the 1949 trial in New York, Davis recounted his conversion to Communism during the Herndon trial in Atlanta. He mentioned the witness who had referred to Herndon as a "darkey" and stressed that Communism offered him a way to help his race.[36]

Davis denied that the party advocated violent overthrow of the government but insisted that blacks in the South had the right to self-determination.

The trial lasted nine months. The judge, Harold R. Medina, agreed with prosecutors that the freedom of speech guaranteed by the Constitution was not absolute but could be limited if there was "sufficient danger of the overthrow of the government."

The jury convicted all eleven Communists. Ben Davis was expelled from the New York City Council. After exhausting his appeals, he found himself behind bars, serving a five-year sentence in a bleak federal prison in Terre Haute, Indiana.[37]

CHAPTER 10

The
UPRISING

The conviction and imprisonment of Benjamin Davis and the other party leaders effectively made it illegal to be a Communist in the United States—or at least to be a Communist who operated in the open and discussed or proposed radical ideas such as black nationhood.

In 1937, the United States Supreme Court had struck down Angelo Herndon's conviction, ruling that Georgia was using its insurrection law as nothing more than a "dragnet" to snare anyone who "agitates for a change of government."

And that was exactly what the federal government was now doing with the Smith Act. It would only get worse in 1949, after the Soviet Union detonated a nuclear bomb and the Communists gained control of China. The reaction in the United States can accurately be described as hysteria, as the Red Scare encompassed virtually every aspect of life and ran roughshod over the Constitution. The Cold War's hot spots included Korea, where the United States would fight Chinese soldiers on the ground and Russian pilots in the air.

There was palpable fear in the United States of international Communism. Politicians including Richard Nixon and Senator Joseph McCarthy would capitalize on it for political gain.

Soviet espionage was a fact of life in the United States particularly during World War II, when the Americans and Soviets were military allies and the United States, like other countries, was working furiously to develop an atomic bomb. But if the previous two decades were any indication, there was little, if any, threat of a Communist uprising, militant or otherwise, in America, as compared to China, Greece, Vietnam, and other countries. Nor was there much chance that Communists would attract anything close to the double-digit numbers at the ballot box that Richard Wright had witnessed in Europe.

"The people know Soviet communism," Supreme Court justice William O. Douglas wrote in his dissent to the court's 1951 decision upholding Benjamin Davis's conviction and those of the other Communist leaders. "The doctrine of Soviet communism is exposed in all of its ugliness and the American people want none of it."[1]

Still, the Red Scare swept into the rank-and-file population of schoolteachers, factory workers, Hollywood script writers, and other Americans. These people were not charged with espionage. Their only alleged crime was membership in or sympathy for the Communist cause. And the age-old constitutional guarantee that the accused had a right to face their accusers was tossed by the wayside as anonymous informant after anonymous informant pointed fingers at coworkers and neighbors in a fashion that at times resembled the Soviet purges of the 1930s and beyond. Douglas called the Red Scare a "witch hunt." It was jailing Communists, yes, but at the same time was chipping away at the First Amendment rights of everyone else.

On June 19, 1953, the United States executed Julius and Ethel Rosenberg for espionage. Any notions of their innocence were dispelled with the publication of *The Haunted Wood*, a book that quoted Soviet documents confirming that the Rosenbergs were indeed Soviet espionage agents. In fact, Julius Rosenberg was so successful an agent that he supervised other United States operatives, the documents said. Julius and Ethel recruited her brother, David Greenglass, to help the Soviets spy on the American program to develop an atomic bomb. David Greenglass was in a strong position to do so as a United States Army sergeant working at the Los Alamos National Laboratory, where the Manhattan Project was under way.[2] It is debatable, however, whether information provided by Greenglass really helped the Soviets or simply affirmed information they already had.

Regardless, a serious legal question lingered over whether the Rosenbergs should have been put to death.

Two days before they were scheduled to die in the electric chair, Douglas issued a stay to explore whether or not the law allowed the death penalty in their case. The problem was this: Congress in 1946 had changed the Atomic Energy Act to allow death sentences only if recommended by the jury. The jury had not recommended death for the Rosenbergs. Instead, the trial judge had imposed it on the assumption that the original version of the law applied, since the

Rosenberg conspiracy was alleged to have taken place from 1944 to 1950. However, according to Douglas, the most incriminating evidence against the Rosenbergs covered events occurring after the law was changed in 1946.

"The question was analogous to the case in which, while a burglar was entering the house, the penalty for burglary was lightened," Douglas wrote. "Which penalty should be applied, the heavier or the lesser one?"[3]

It was a serious legal question, but the United States was in a state of anti-Communist hysteria. "If you issue the Rosenbergs a stay, there will be a lynching party waiting for you here," said a telegram from Douglas's hometown of Yakima, Washington, where he was headed for the summer recess.[4]

A stay would have provided federal district and appellate courts time to review the legal question so that the Supreme Court could look at it again in the fall. "No harm would be done," Douglas said. "The Rosenbergs were behind bars. They could be executed in October as well as in June."

But Fred Vinson, chief justice of the Supreme Court, convened a special term of court, and the justices overturned the stay issued by Douglas. The Rosenbergs died that night in the electric chair at New York's Sing Sing prison. "When that happened, the people of this country experienced a thrill," Douglas later wrote.[5]

Yet in the middle of this conservative Cold War decade, the Supreme Court, in the most significant civil rights ruling of the twentieth century, outlawed separate schools for blacks and whites. The unanimous ruling in *Brown v. Board of Education* was issued less than a year after the Rosenbergs were executed. It overturned the "separate but equal" doctrine endorsed by the court in 1896. Among the justices to vote for integrating the schools was Hugo Black of Alabama, a former member of the Ku Klux Klan and now one of the most liberal justices.

This was the NAACP's case. The group had been often criticized by the Communists for acting too slowly and being too conservative. The Supreme Court, hoping to avoid a complete upheaval of Southern society, allowed states to approach school integration "with all deliberate speed." The process would drag on for decades.

But the *Brown* case would directly lead a year later to the first true uprising in the American South—the uprising the Communists had tried for decades to incite, without success.

Rosa Parks was a black seamstress in Montgomery, Alabama. But she was more than that. She was a longtime civil rights activist and secretary at the local NAACP branch. Her activist roots stretched back to the Scottsboro case. Parks's husband, Raymond, had helped raise money for the Scottsboro defense early in the case, when it was still controlled by the Communists.

"Whites accused anybody who was working for black people with being a communist," Rosa Parks wrote in her memoirs. "But I don't think anyone in [Raymond] Parks' group was a communist."[6] Her husband would not allow Rosa to attend the meetings, believing it was too dangerous. But in 1946, Rosa worked to free one of the Scottsboro defendants, Andy Wright, who had been put back in prison for leaving the state while on parole.

In the summer of 1955, Parks spent ten days at the Highlander School in Tennessee attending workshops, mostly on school desegregation, which was on the horizon following the *Brown* decision. After *Brown*, the Montgomery NAACP was actively looking for a test case to challenge segregation on buses as well, the door having been opened to challenge all separate-but-equal accommodations. When a black Montgomery teenager named Claudette Colvin was arrested in the spring of 1955 for refusing to move to the back of the bus, the NAACP thought it had just the right person for a challenge, until it was discovered that Colvin was pregnant but not married.

On December 1, 1955, Parks, forty-two, was arrested for the same thing, but not because she wanted to be the test case to challenge segregated buses. "I saw a vacant seat in the middle section of the bus and I took it," Rosa remembered.[7]

She was actually sitting in the front row of the black section of the bus, which was not against the rules. It did not pose a problem until the next stop, when several white passengers boarded, filling up all the white seats and leaving one white passenger standing. Under the rules of segregation, once the white section was filled, blacks were required to give up their seats in the black section to accommodate them, even if that meant standing.

The bus driver demanded that Parks and three other black passengers give up their seats. Rosa refused.

"Well, I'm going to have you arrested," the driver said.

"You may do so," Rosa replied calmly.

Every revolution requires a hero. The American Communists never really had one. Herbert Newton was brave, venturing into the hostile South in 1930 and attempting to speak in favor of Communism in a biracial group in the middle of downtown Atlanta. Angelo Herndon was equally brave, organizing whites and blacks to demand relief funds in the midst of the Great Depression. Both were imprisoned and jailed and faced the death penalty. But they remained obscure figures, never capturing the kind of widespread fame or the following that would inspire a mass uprising.

That was not the case with Rosa Parks.

After her arrest, the NAACP immediately called for a boycott of the private bus system and enlisted support from the churches in Montgomery, a great organizational asset that never would have been available to the atheistic Communists.

Eighteen ministers met across from the Alabama Capitol at Dexter Avenue Baptist Church, whose minister was twenty-six-year-old Martin Luther King Jr. King was a Morehouse College man recruited in 1944 while still in high school by Benjamin Mays, the college president. Morehouse was losing so many of its students to military service during World War II that it had to recruit high-school students to stay afloat. King was from a prominent family in Atlanta. His father, Martin Luther King Sr., was pastor of Ebenezer Baptist Church and a Morehouse trustee.

Throughout decades of living under segregation, Mays had been quietly resisting. He would take stairs instead of segregated elevators. More than a decade before Rosa Parks refused to give up her seat on a Montgomery bus, Mays filed a complaint with the Interstate Commerce Commission against Southern Railway after an angry steward forced him to give up his seat in the white section of a dining car. There was no place for Mays to sit, since four white soldiers were at the table reserved for black passengers.[8]

Mays realized that the Communist Party and a new generation of black writers including Richard Wright were competing for the hearts and minds of African Americans, and that the black church, in order to remain relevant, would have to offer more than just the prospect of going to heaven. It had to confront problems in the here and now, including racism, poverty, and disenfranchisement. Mays believed that change was possible, and preferable, through nonviolent, democratic means, and not by forming a new black nation or by transforming the United States into a Soviet puppet state.

Mays met with Indian leader Mahatma Gandhi in late 1936, the same year Jane and Herbert Newton were in the Soviet Union on an extended trip. He had also seen firsthand the power of democracy through the ballot box. In the early 1920s, Atlanta had no black high school. The local black colleges and universities, including Morehouse, offered their own high-school programs. It was at Morehouse where Benjamin Davis attended high school before going on to Amherst and Harvard. Blacks were outlawed from voting in the crucial Democratic Party primary but were not barred from casting ballots in municipal bond referendums. It was not until black voters helped defeat a school bond referendum that the Atlanta school board decided to build the city's first black high school, Booker T. Washington, in 1924. There was indeed black power at the ballot box decades before the civil rights movement began.

As a Morehouse student, Martin Luther King Jr. had attended Mays's Tuesday-morning chapel services and often lingered to discuss the sermon, "usually with approval but sometimes questioning or disagreeing."[9]

King's career path was similar to that of his mentor,

Mays: undergraduate degree, Ph.D. in theology, Baptist minister. As King was finishing up his doctorate at Boston College, Mays tried to hire him on the Morehouse faculty, but the young minister decided instead to take the pulpit at Dexter Avenue Baptist.

At a meeting of the Montgomery Improvement Association, a group formed after Rosa Parks's arrest, King emerged as the leader of the new boycott movement. His first speech was thundering and powerful. He was arguably among the best orators in the world.

"There comes a time when people get tired," King said. "We are here this evening to say to those who have mistreated us so long that we are tired—tired of being segregated and humiliated; tired of being kicked around by the brutal feet of oppression."[10]

He received loud cheers and amens. A massive boycott was on that would eventually shut down the bus system. It was boosted by the massive organizational powers of the NAACP and churches, which launched ride-share programs, purchased vans, and even obtained insurance for the vehicles through Lloyd's of London after local white agents refused to provide coverage.

King would later describe the Montgomery bus boycott as "the first flash of organized, sustained mass action and nonviolent revolt against the Southern way of life." The uprising was finally here. It was nonviolent.[11]

By contrast, Communist protests in the United States frequently devolved into brawls, demonstrators and policemen alike ending up bruised, battered, and sometimes killed. For example, a Communist-led strike at a textile mill in Gastonia, North Carolina, in 1929 had ended up with one of the strikers and the police chief, Orville Aderholt, shot dead.

The nonviolence of the Montgomery boycott was motivated by the concept of Christian love, King later wrote. "It was the Sermon on the Mount, rather than a doctrine of passive resistance, that initially inspired the Negros of Montgomery to dignified social action," said King.

Early on, however, Juliette Morgan, a white woman who sympathized with the boycott, wrote a letter to the editor of the *Montgomery Advertiser* comparing the protest to Gandhi's movement in India.[12]

King realized that combining Christian love and Gandhi's method of nonviolence would be the most powerful approach in Montgomery. "In other words, Christ furnished the spirit and motivation while Gandhi furnished the method," said King.

Meanwhile, it was Benjamin Mays, the man who had actually met Gandhi, who helped keep King in Montgomery as white opposition stiffened and police began indicting and arresting boycotters.

King was among the hundred people indicted under an old Alabama law outlawing boycotts. He was in Nashville giving a speech when the indictment was returned. On his way back to Montgomery, he stopped off in Atlanta, where his father convened a council of elders to discuss whether or not King should return to Montgomery and face arrest. The senior King told the advisors that he didn't think Martin should go back to Montgomery. There was a murmur of agreement in the group—except for one man, Benjamin Mays.

"I looked at Dr. Mays, one of the great influences of my life," King wrote. "Perhaps he heard my unspoken plea. At any rate, he was soon defending my position strongly. The others joined him in supporting me."[13]

In Montgomery, King reported to jail, along with other indicted boycotters. "An almost holiday atmosphere prevailed." A once "fear ridden people" were now proud to be arrested for the cause of freedom, King said.

There were fearful times in the boycott, such as when the porch of King's home was bombed and a stick of dynamite was thrown on the lawn of the former local NAACP director, E. D. Nixon. The officers of King's church urged him to hire armed security guards. King applied for a permit to carry a gun in his car, which, not surprisingly, was denied by the local sheriff's department. King already had one gun in his home but in the end decided that, as the leader of a non-violent movement, he could not justify using firearms even for his own protection. Instead, he installed floodlights at his home, hired unarmed watchmen, and promised never to drive alone.[14]

In her memoirs, Rosa Parks wrote that "to this day, I am not an absolute supporter of nonviolence in all situations. But I strongly believe that the civil rights movement of the 1950s and 1960s could not have been successful without Dr. King and his firm belief in nonviolence."[15]

The boycott lasted for more than a year, but it did not desegregate the buses. Rather, the Supreme Court did, upholding a lower federal court ruling in favor of black Montgomery bus riders who had challenged segregation. The ruling outlawed segregated public transportation in the same way *Brown* had outlawed separate schools for blacks and whites.

Although it was in the courts where the ultimate legal victory arrived, the boycotters had proven, King pointed out, that they could mount a sustained fight against segregation, not giving up until they met their objectives. The boycott launched the civil rights movement, and many more landmark victories would follow.

Harry Haywood, the first African American to endorse a separate black nation in the American South, was not impressed. He saw King ultimately as a sellout who represented not the masses but the black middle class. "Even the victories that were won in desegregation and legal reforms produced no improvement in the conditions of poor and working-class blacks," Haywood wrote in his 1978 memoirs.

Only with "organized, armed self defense" could blacks truly overcome white suppression in the Deep South, said Haywood. The Civil Rights Act of 1964 was designed to "get the Black Movement off the Street and back into the courtroom," he said.[16]

In the end, the Communist Party had missed its chance at revolution by giving up too early on black nationhood, Haywood wrote. If only the party had stuck to the cause, it would have been in place to seize the day in the 1950s and 1960s when the civil rights movement finally emerged, Haywood believed.

But the goals of the Communists and those of Martin Luther King and his supporters were completely different. The Communists advocated a complete upheaval of all aspects of American society. This was the only way to create a truly fair, race-blind society, they believed. Half-measures and piecemeal court victories would not be enough.

In 1949, King had read Karl Marx extensively, trying to understand the appeal of Communism. He found it not only secularist, having "no place for God," but utterly materialistic, focusing on human possessions, not the spirit. "History is ultimately guided by spirit, not matter," King wrote.[17]

King, like Richard Wright and most Americans of all races, valued basic American freedoms of speech and thought—the right to say what one wanted, think what one wanted, read what one chose. The civil rights movement was about expanding those freedoms, not limiting them, as the Communists wanted to do. "Man is not made for the state," said King. "The state is made for man."[18]

In his position on freedom and Communism, King was very much in sync with mainstream white America. Few Americans, white or black, seemed to care much for the Communists.

Benjamin Mays, who endured a lifetime of racial discrimination, traveled the world during his career as an educator and minister. He knew America's flaws as well as anyone, but Mays would not endorse Communism or black nationhood. "I have concluded that the United States, despite all its imperfections, is the best country for me," said Mays. "My job is to continue the battle to make America in reality what it claims to be."

The question facing the black man in America, Mays wrote, was "what [can he] do to enlarge his own freedom, to create in himself a sense of his inherent self worth and to develop economic and political security?"[19]

The Communists offered African Americans the prospect of their own nation, and they rejected it. Even many Communists finally conceded that African Americans were part of the fabric of America.

While the way out of racism would not be easy, Mays concluded, it would be a journey that blacks and whites took together. That much had been decided.

"Whatever the future holds for the American people," Mays wrote, "it must be accepted that the United States belongs to the black man as much as to the white man."[20]

Americans were all in this together, Mays believed.

EPILOGUE

Richard Wright died in Paris in 1960, a bitter man.

While blacks and whites in the United States were fighting it out in the streets and in the courts over race and civil rights, Wright's solution had been to escape racism by walking away.

He was euphoric living in France as a wealthy man, no longer subject to American racism. But the distance hurt his career as a pioneering writer on American race. At the time of his death, he was, his critics both black and white said, detached, out of touch with America.

In February 1959, four years after the Montgomery bus boycott had begun, Martin Luther King Jr. and his wife, Coretta, stopped by Wright's spacious apartment on Rue Monsieur le Prince in Paris. The Kings were on their way to visit India at the invitation of Prime Minister Jawaharlal Nehru. Lawrence Reddick, an African American historian and a friend of Wright's, was on the trip with the Kings and suggested they pay a visit.

"Wright brought us up to date on European attitudes on the Negro question and gave us a taste of the best French cooking," King recalled.[1]

Wright introduced King to his daughter, Julia, and asked the civil rights leader to show her his scar. The previous year, King had been holding a book signing in a Harlem department store when a deranged woman stabbed him in the chest, nearly killing him.

Wright was still technically married to Ellen, but she was living in England and he in France. The Wrights eventually gave up both their expensive apartment in Paris and their farmhouse in Normandy. As Wright's career faltered, so did his health. He suffered from amoebic dysentery, which he may have contracted on trips to Africa or even from his childhood in Mississippi. Many suspected it was the treatment, not the dysentery, that eventually killed him at age fifty-two.

At the end of his life, Wright, like some of the former Communist comrades he had come to despise, was underwhelmed by the progress of race relations in the United States. Six years after *Brown v. Board of Education*, only a small percentage of black students were in white schools, Wright told French reporters. "A black child cannot enter the American school system without being crucified psychologically," he said.[2]

In a "long, rambling, bitter speech" less than a month before he died, Wright attacked his own race, including fellow black artists and intellectuals, whom he said were constantly trying to destroy each other with their jealousy, rivalry, and infighting. Most of the black churches, Wright said, had turned on singer and actor Paul Robeson when he became a Communist, refusing to attend any event at which Robeson was present. "The hand of the white man was effective but invisible," Wright said, failing to mention that he himself had also strongly and powerfully rejected the Communists.[3]

When blacks rioted across the United States in the 1960s, some said Wright's prediction of a violent revolution against white racism had finally come to pass. But Wright did not predict that much of the destruction would be inwardly directed—that it would be African American neighborhoods, not white ones, that would burn. And even Wright probably would have been surprised that there would still be race riots in the United States in 2015, or that the South Side of Chicago, Bigger Thomas country, would remain a hotbed of black-on-black murder. Or that huge racial issues such as police brutality and mass incarceration would continue to fester in the United States. Or that in 2013, the average wealth of black households would be just $11,000, compared to $141,900 for white households, a staggering disparity.[4] Or that Wright's own phrase in *Native Son*, "the crime of being black," would still be around in different iterations, including "driving while black," "Tasered while black," and "shot while black."

When Benjamin Davis died in New York in 1964, he was still a leader of the American Communist Party and still under federal indictment, despite having served more than three years in prison in the 1950s on the 1949 Smith Act conviction. At his death, Davis was awaiting trial for failing to register the party as an agent of the Soviet Union under the

McCarran Act. Davis defended the Soviet Union until the end, even after many of the abuses of the Stalin era had come to light.[5]

Three years after Davis's death, the *New York Times* carried on its front page a story that the eighteen-year-old daughter of United States secretary of state Dean Rusk had married a black man.[6] Rusk, the article said, had offered to resign if the wedding caused a controversy for President Lyndon Johnson, who was busy waging war against the Communists in Vietnam. When Rusk left the administration to take a teaching position at the University of Georgia Law School, a Georgia politician named Roy Harris objected to the appointment, citing the interracial marriage. This was more than three decades after Jane and Herbert Newton had married.

Martin Luther King Jr., like Gandhi, would die from an assassin's bullet. King, sensing perhaps that he would die before the much older Mays, had asked his mentor to give his eulogy, which Mays delivered on April 9, 1968.

After her divorce from Herbert Newton, Jane found herself in 1963 as the city clerk of Santa Barbara. The United States had not yet had its fill of persecuting and prosecuting Communists, so Jane kept a low profile. She never remarried.[7]

In 1974, Santa Barbara became Ronald Reagan country. The Republican governor of California purchased a ranch there that would become the Western White House during his presidency. One of Jane's grandsons would later become a spokesman for another Republican, Alaska governor and 2008 vice presidential nominee Sarah Palin.

Jane, a longtime smoker and drinker, died on August 19,

1982. On Communism, Jane had been on the wrong side of history. But on race in America, she was decades ahead of her time.

Her father, former American Legion commander John Garfield Emery, had been laid to rest as a war hero at Arlington National Cemetery. But Jane did not like funerals. So after she died, there was none.

ACKNOWLEDGMENTS

Special thanks to my family for their support. I especially thank my wife, Susan, who found this story during one of many trips to a dark and lonely archive, and my son Zachary, for his feedback and editing.

Dolores Newton, daughter of Jane and Herbert Newton, spent hours with me on the telephone and sent me many invaluable documents that allowed me to better understand her parents' lives and story. I sincerely appreciate her help.

Thanks to all the archivists along the way, especially V. N. Shepelev, deputy director of the Russian archives in Moscow, who retrieved Herbert Newton's file for me.

Dr. Woodford McClellan, professor emeritus at the University of Virginia, spent many long hours translating the documents and helping me understand them, as did Athan Biss, a graduate student at the University of Wisconsin.

Thanks as well to Steve Kirk and Carolyn Sakowski and all the staff at John F. Blair, Publisher, for believing in the book and shaping it along the way.

NOTES

PROLOGUE

[1] Richard Wright, *Native Son* (New York: Harper & Brothers, 1940), 296.

[2] Michel Fabre to Jane Newton, Jan. 2, 1963. Courtesy of Dolores Newton.

[3] Michel Fabre to Jane Newton, Jan. 21, 1963. Courtesy of Dolores Newton.

[4] Jane Newton to Michel Fabre, Jan. 21, 1964. Courtesy of Dolores Newton.

[5] Jane Newton, notes for undated third letter to Michel Fabre.

CHAPTER 1

[1] "Respect to Flag Civic Duty, Says Legion Chieftain," *Grand Rapids Press*, June 21, 1921, 12.

[2] Advertisement, *Grand Rapids Press*, March 6, 1915, 13. "Don't employ a novice if you don't want ruined walls," Emery told customers.

[3] Jane Newton, "Problem Girls Tell Life Story," *Chicago Times*, six-part autobiographical series, Dec. 1934.

[4] *Ibid*.

[5] "Welcome Home," *Grand Rapids Press*, Oct. 17, 1919, 14.

[6] "Legion Founders Meet Here Again," *New York Times*, Aug. 28, 1947, 2.

[7] "The Citizen Veteran," *Portland Oregonian*, July 3, 1921, 2.

[8] Newton, "Problem Girls."

[9] *Ibid*.

[10] *Ibid.*

[11] Robert Burns, *I Am a Fugitive from a Georgia Chain Gang!* (Athens: University of Georgia Press, 1997).

[12] Harry Haywood, *Black Communist in the Freedom Struggle: The Life of Harry Haywood*, ed. by Gwendolyn Midlo Hall (reprint, Minneapolis: University of Minnesota Press, 2012), 38.

[13] *Ibid.*, 39.

[14] "Houston Objects to More Negro Troops," *New York Times*, Aug. 27, 1917, 6.

[15] Haywood, *Black Communist*, 41.

[16] *Ibid.*, 44.

[17] *Ibid.*, 48.

[18] "Kreisler Concert Here Is Canceled: American Legion Objects to Appearance of Enemy Alien at Armory," *Grand Rapids Press*, Oct. 27, 1919, 14.

[19] "Texans to Oust and Aid Japanese," *New York Times*, Jan. 9, 1921, 3.

[20] "Legion to Make Drive for Members July 4," *New York Times*, June 17, 1921, 17.

[21] "Legion Warns Harding against Freeing Debs," *New York Times*, July 30, 1921, 10.

[22] "Belgium Honors Legion," *New York Times*, Aug. 29, 1921, 3.

[23] "Emery Faces His Critics," *New York Times*, Sept. 23, 1921, 8.

[24] "Legion Greets Foch with Wild Acclaim," *New York Times*, Nov. 1, 1921, 1.

[25] "Legionnaires Enter Race for Commander," *New York Times*, Oct. 27, 1921, 19.

[26] "What the Constitution Means to Me," *Grand Rapids Press*, June 5, 1922, 2.

27 Newton, "Problem Girls."

28 Allan Seager, "Actress with Red Garters," in *Frieze of Girls: Memoirs as Fiction* (Ann Arbor: University of Michigan Press, 2004). Jane's daughter Dolores Newton referred the author to the story. Although "Actress" is fiction, Dolores believes it to be an accurate portrayal of her mother.

29 Newton, "Problem Girls."

30 *Ibid*.

31 Seager, "Actress with Red Garters," 114.

CHAPTER 2

1 From an autobiographical document in Herbert Newton's file at the Russian archives, document 11972, RGASPI, dated Apr. 16, 1932, marked "Strictly confidential." Over the years, Newton regularly sent slightly varying résumés to the Soviet government.

2 *Ibid*.

3 *Ibid*.

4 Benjamin Mays, *Born to Rebel* (Athens: University of Georgia Press, 1971), 45.

5 *Ibid*.

6 *Ibid*, 28.

7 Joy Gleason Carew, *Blacks, Reds, and Russians: Sojourners in Search of the Soviet Promise* (New Brunswick, NJ: Rutgers University Press, 2008), 18.

8 "Negroes Assail Morocco Fliers," *Boston Herald*, Nov. 1, 1925, 15.

9 "Communist Drive to Rouse Negroes Watched by U.S.," *Washington Evening Star*, Oct. 24, 1925, 1.

10 Autobiographical document in Herbert Newton's file

at Russian archives.

[11] Robert Robinson, *Black on Red* (Acropolis, 1988), 29.

[12] "Negroes," *Boston Herald*, July 17, 1927, 40.

[13] Herbert Newton to his mother, Mary, Nov. 25, 1927. Courtesy of Dolores Newton.

[14] Herbert Newton to his mother, Jan. 9, 1928. Courtesy of Dolores Newton.

[15] Woodford McClellan, "Black Hajj to Red Mecca," in *Africa in Russia, Russia in Africa* (Trenton NJ: Africa World Press, 2007), 61–83.

[16] Herbert Newton to his mother, Jan. 9, 1928.

[17] Haywood, *Black Communist*, 135.

[18] Robinson, *Black on Red*, 66.

[19] Herbert Newton to his mother, Apr. 15, 1929.

[20] *Ibid.*

[21] Haywood, *Black Communist*, 138.

[22] *Ibid.*,139.

[23] Glenda Elizabeth Gilmore, *Defying Dixie* (New York: W. W. Norton, 2008), 53.

[24] Ibid., 59.

[25] Herbert Newton to his mother, Aug. 21, 1928.

[26] B. D. Wolfe to the Central Control Commission of the Communist Party of the Soviet Union, Feb. 14, 1929, document in Herbert Newton's file at the Russian archives.

[27] Haywood, *Black Communist*, 160.

[28] Herbert Newton to Klavdiia Kirsanova, May 14, 1930, in Herbert Newton's file at the Russian archives.

CHAPTER 3

[1] Herbert Newton to his mother, May 14, 1930.

[2] Emily Woodward, *Empire: Georgia Today in Pictures and*

Paragraphs (Atlanta: Ruralist Press, 1936), 23.

[3] Herbert Newton to his mother, May 14, 1930.

[4] *Ibid*.

[5] Mays, *Born to Rebel*, 36.

[6] Randal Maurice Jelks, *Schoolmaster of the Movement* (Chapel Hill: University of North Carolina Press, 2012), 25.

[7] Untitled article, *Labor Defender* newspaper, Aug. 1930.

[8] *Ibid*.

[9] Anne Burlak's unpublished memoirs, Neilson Library, Smith College.

[10] *Ibid*.

[11] Untitled article, *Labor Defender*, Aug. 1930.

[12] Anne Burlak's unpublished memoirs.

[13] *Ibid*.

[14] "Widow of Fain Loses Fight to Get Insurance," *Atlanta Constitution*, Apr. 25, 1940, 2.

[15] Anne Burlak's unpublished memoirs.

[16] *Ibid*.

[17] *Ibid*.

[18] Herbert Newton to his mother, June 17, 1930. Courtesy of Dolores Newton.

[19] Indictment 37299, attempting to incite insurrection, Fulton County Superior Court, May 21, 1930.

[20] Herbert Newton to his mother, July 1, 1930.

[21] Herbert Newton, "Georgia Tops the List in Lynchings," *Liberator*, undated, in Newton's file, Communist Party of the United States.

[22] "Ask Free Speech for Reds," *New York Times*, Aug. 4, 1930, 4.

[23] Anne Burlak's unpublished memoirs.

CHAPTER 4

[1] "Reds Here Orderly at Sacco Meeting," *New York Times*, Aug. 23, 1930, 2.

[2] Haywood, *Black Communist*, 163.

[3] "'Invasion' of Reds Quickly Dispersed," *New York Times*, Dec. 2, 1930, 1.

[4] Newton, "Problem Girls."

[5] Seager, "Actress with Red Garters," 108.

[6] Newton, "Problem Girls."

[7] *Ibid.*

[8] "Text of the U.S. Supreme Court in the Scottsboro Case," *New York Times*, Nov. 8, 1932.

[9] *Ibid.*

[10] Dan T. Carter, *Scottsboro: A Tragedy of the American South*, rev. ed. (Baton Rouge: Louisiana State University Press, 1979), 181.

[11] "Hunger Army Battles Police," *Chicago Defender*, Jan. 16, 1932, 1.

[12] *Ibid.*

[13] Newton, "Problem Girls."

[14] Mays, *Born to Rebel*, 229.

[15] Newton, "Problem Girls."

[16] *Ibid.*

CHAPTER 5

[1] Angelo Herndon, *Let Me Live* (Arno Press and *New York Times*, 1969), 175.

[2] "Black Shirt Meeting Dispersed, Eight Jailed," *Atlanta Constitution*, June 1, 1932, 20.

[3] "Everything Is Peaches Down in Georgia," *Daily Worker*, July 8, 1932, 6.

[4] "Talented Atlanta Children to Appear in Mammoth Revue," *Atlanta Constitution*, Feb. 28, 1932, 6.

[5] "Sound Reconstruction," *Atlanta Constitution*, Aug. 26, 1932, 10.

[6] "Room for 20 Families on Farm," *Atlanta Daily World*, Sept. 14, 1932, 1.

[7] "No Action Taken by County Board on Tax for Needy," *Atlanta Constitution*, June 26, 1932, 1.

[8] "Funds Exhausted," *Atlanta Constitution*, June 17, 1932, 1.

[9] Herndon, *Let Me Live*, 26.

[10] *Ibid.*, 8.

[11] Trial transcript, *State v. Angelo Herndon*, case 37-182, Fulton County Superior Court, 115, available at Georgia archives.

[12] *Ibid.*, 191.

[13] "Bar Negroes from Relief Meeting," *Atlanta Daily World*, June 30, 1932, 1.

[14] "County Provides $6,000 for Needy," *Atlanta Constitution*, July 2, 1932, 1.

[15] Herndon trial transcript, 114.

[16] *Ibid.*, 110.

[17] *Ibid.*, 33.

[18] *Ibid.*, 34.

[19] *Ibid.*, 20.

[20] *Ibid.*, 115.

[21] *Ibid.*, Herndon indictment included in trial transcript.

[22] "Angelo Herndon Case Will Close," *Macon Telegraph*, July 23, 1937, 13.

[23] Benjamin J. Davis, *Communist Councilman from Harlem* (International Publishers Co., 1969), 156.

[24] Herndon trial transcript, 95.

[25] *Ibid.*, 114.

[26] *Ibid.*

[27] *Ibid.*, 127.

[28] *Ibid.*, 143.

[29] *Ibid.* Herndon's testimony begins on 129.

[30] Charles H. Martin, *The Angelo Herndon Case and Southern Justice* (Baton Rouge: Louisiana State University Press, 1976), 57.

[31] *Ibid.*, 59.

[32] Burns, *I Am a Fugitive*, 59.

[33] "As Others See It," *Macon Telegraph*, Jan. 23, 1933.

[34] Herndon trial transcript, 201.

[35] Davis, *Communist Councilman from Harlem*, 75.

CHAPTER 6

[1] "Communists Storm De Priest Mass Meeting," *Chicago Defender*, Nov. 5, 1932, 13.

[2] "Pass De Priest Resolution," *New York Times*, June 26, 1929, 9.

[3] "Police Check Reds' Attack on De Priest," *Chicago Defender*, July 23, 1932, 1.

[4] "Communists Storm De Priest Mass Meeting."

[5] "Reds Storm City in Food Plea," *Chicago Defender*, Nov. 5, 1932, 1.

[6] "Chicago Negroes Remain with GOP," *Atlanta Daily World*, Nov. 14, 1932, 2.

[7] James G. Ryan, *Earl Browder: The Failure of American Communism*, 2nd ed. (Tuscaloosa: University of Alabama Press, 1997), 82.

[8] *Ibid.*, 83.

[9] Newton, "Problem Girls."

[10] *Ibid*.

[11] Jane Newton to Michel Fabre, Jan. 21, 1964.

[12] Newton, "Problem Girls."

[13] Jane Newton to Michel Fabre, Jan. 21, 1964.

[14] "White Family Fight Cause of Family Eviction," *Chicago Defender*, Dec. 1, 1934, 4.

[15] "Eviction of Family Caused Solely by Race Prejudice," *Chicago Defender*, Dec. 15, 1934, 2.

[16] "Drama in Court Bares Tragedy of Woman Red," *Chicago Tribune*, Dec. 16, 1934, 3.

[17] "Daughter of Old American Family Found Wed to Negro Communist," *Canton Repository* newspaper, Dec. 16, 1934, 28.

[18] Benjamin Harris and Fran Brotherton, "Communism, Miscegenation, and *Dementia Simplex*: The Trials of Jane Emery Newton," unpublished manuscript, 1993. Courtesy of Benjamin Harris.

[19] "Drama in Court Bares Tragedy of Woman Red."

[20] "Large Inheritances Don't Spell Security," *Omaha World Herald*, Nov. 22, 1948, 6.

[21] "Drinking Gains among Women," *Trenton* (NJ) *Evening Times*, May 15, 1946, 8.

[22] Harris and Brotherton, "Communism, Miscegenation."

[23] *Ibid*.

[24] *Ibid*.

[25] Newton, "Problem Girls."

[26] "Thoughts in Passing," *Chicago Defender*, Dec. 22, 1934, 10.

[27] "Race Prejudice Not a Natural State," *Chicago Defender*, Jan. 5, 1935, 5.

[28] "Mrs. Jane Newton Sane, Alienists Find," *Chicago Defender*, Dec. 19, 1934, 5.

[29] *Ibid*.

[30] Newton, "Problem Girls."

[31] *Ibid*.

[32] W. A. S. Douglas, "Found Sane, Mrs. Newton Rejoins Reds," unidentified newspaper clipping in Claude A. Barnett Papers, Fort Valley State University archives.

CHAPTER 7

[1] "Daughter of General Defends Communist," *Register-Republic* (Rockford, IL), March 13, 1935, 8.

[2] "Deny Jim Crowism at University of Chicago," *Kansas City Plaindealer*, March 22, 1935.

[3] "Detroit Paper Stirred over Newtons' Visit," *Chicago Defender*, March 2, 1935, 4.

[4] Jane Newton to Michel Fabre, Jan. 21, 1964.

[5] Richard Wright, *Black Boy* (New York: Harper & Brothers, 1945; reprint, First Perennial Classics, 1998), 330.

[6] Jane Newton to Michel Fabre, Jan. 21, 1964.

[7] Wright, *Black Boy*, 331.

[8] Jane Newton to Michel Fabre, Jan. 21, 1964.

[9] "Communists Storm De Priest Mass Meeting."

[10] Wright, *Black Boy*, 352. In the book, Wright calls Haywood "Buddy Nealson."

[11] Jane Newton to Michel Fabre, Jan. 21, 1964.

[12] *Ibid*.

[13] Newton's Profintern membership is confirmed in documents in his file at the Russian archives.

[14] "Red Group in WPA Stirs Discontent," *New York Times*, Apr. 14, 1936, 1.

[15] Wright, *Black Boy*, 376.

[16] From documents in Herbert Newton's file at the Russian archives.

[17] "J. E. Newton off to Russia," *Kansas City Plaindealer*, June 5, 1936, 23.

[18] Dolores Newton, interview with the author, Sept. 2012.

[19] From documents in Herbert Newton's file at the Russian archives.

[20] Robinson, *Black on Red*, 122.

[21] Ryan, *Earl Browder*, 105.

[22] *Ibid.*, 268.

[23] McClellan, "Black Hajj to Red Mecca."

[24] Haywood, *Black Communist*, 242.

[25] Mays, *Born to Rebel*, 158.

[26] *Ibid.*, 155.

CHAPTER 8

[1] Herndon, *Let Me Live*, 296.

[2] Jane Newton to Michel Fabre, Feb. 26, 1964.

[3] *Herndon v. Lowry*, 301 U.S. 242-78 (1937).

[4] Carter, *Scottsboro*, 313.

[5] Hazel Rowley, *The Life and Times of Richard Wright* (Chicago: University of Chicago Press, 2001), 122.

[6] *Ibid.*, 129.

[7] Jane Newton to Michel Fabre, Feb. 26, 1964.

[8] *Ibid.*

[9] Wright, *Native Son*.

[10] Richard Wright, *How Bigger Was Born* (New York: Harper & Brothers, 1940), included as appendix to *Native Son*, First Perennial Classics Edition, 1998, 438.

[11] *Ibid.*

[12] Jane Newton to Michel Fabre, Feb. 26, 1964.

[13] *Ibid.*

[14] Wright, Richard, *Native Son* (New York: Harper & Brothers, 1940, First Perennial Classic Edition, 1998), 66.

[15] *Ibid.*, 68

[16] *Ibid.*, 67.

[17] *Ibid.*, 77.

[18] Jane Newton to Michel Fabre, Feb. 26, 1964.

[19] *Ibid.*

[20] *Ibid.*

[21] Fredric Wertham, notes on Richard Wright, Fredric Wertham Papers, Library of Congress.

[22] Jane Newton to Michel Fabre, Feb. 26, 1964.

CHAPTER 9

[1] Jane Newton to Michel Fabre, Feb. 26, 1964.

[2] *Ibid.*

[3] *Ibid.*

[4] Rowley, *Life and Times of Richard Wright*, 191.

[5] Sterling North to Ramona Herdman, Feb. 8, 1940, Wright Papers, Box 103, Beinecke Rare Book and Manuscript Library, Yale University.

[6] Edith Webber to Ramona Herdman, undated, Wright Papers, Box 103, Beinecke Rare Book and Manuscript Library, Yale University.

[7] Wright, *How Bigger Was Born.*

[8] Rowley, *Life and Times of Richard Wright*, 200.

[9] Ben Davis to Richard Wright, Apr. 17, 1940, Wright Papers, Box 96, Beinecke Rare Book and Manuscript Library Yale University.

[10] Rowley, *Life and Times of Richard Wright*, 551.

[11] *Ibid.*, 200.

[12] *Ibid.*

[13] Richard Wright to Margaret Walker, undated, Jackson State University archives.

[14] Edward C. Aswell to Richard Wright, June 12, 1940, Wright Papers, Box 103, Beinecke Rare Book and Manuscript Library, Yale University.

[15] William James Fadiman to Paul Reynolds, Sept. 26, 1939, Wright Papers, Box 103, Beinecke Rare Book and Manuscript Library, Yale University.

[16] Ben Davis to Richard Wright, Oct. 16, 1941, Wright Papers, Box 96, Beinecke Rare Book and Manuscript Library, Yale University.

[17] Rowley, *Life and Times of Richard Wright*, 231.

[18] "29 Pickets Seized at Mayor's Home," *New York Times*, July 19, 1941, 15.

[19] Rowley, *Life and Times of Richard Wright*, 255.

[20] "40 Quit Police Inquiry," *New York Times*, Oct. 3, 1941, 25.

[21] "Picketing Teacher Guilty of Assault," *New York Times*, Nov. 20, 1941, 33.

[22] Richard Wright to Fredric Wertham, Dec. 7, 1941, Fredric Wertham Research Files, Richard Wright Correspondence, 1941–1968, Box 67, Folder 7, Library of Congress.

[23] "Police Beater Is Sentenced," *New York Times*, Dec. 9, 1941, 34.

[24] Dolores Newton, interview with the author, Sept. 2012.

[25] "Leftist School Will Close Soon," *New York Times*, Nov. 28, 1956, 6.

[26] Dolores Newton, interview with the author, Sept. 2012.

[27] *Ibid.*

[28] "Negro Soviet Plan Revived by Davis," *New York Times*, July 24, 1945, 24.

[29] "Harlem Group Scores Davis on Soviet Plan," *New York Times*, July 25, 1941, 14.

[30] "Bail Set at $5,000," *New York Times*, July 21, 1948, 1.

[31] Rowley, *Life and Times of Richard Wright*, 297.

[32] Richard Wright to Fredric Wertham, May 19, 1946, Fredric Wertham Research Files, Richard Wright Correspondence, 1941–1968, Box 67, Folder 7, Library of Congress.

[33] Richard Wright to Fredric Wertham, Oct. 6, 1946, Fredric Wertham Research Files, Richard Wright Correspondence, 1941–1968, Box 67, Folder 7, Library of Congress.

[34] Allen Weinstein and Alexander Vassiliev, *The Haunted Wood* (New York: Random House, 1999), 85.

[35] "Plan for Negro Nation in U.S. Is Told by Red Trial Witness," *New York Times*, Apr. 19, 1949, 1.

[36] "Davis Joins Reds to Help His People," *New York Times*, July 8, 1949, 3.

[37] Davis, *Communist Councilman from Harlem*, 19.

CHAPTER 10

[1] William O. Douglas, *The Court Years: 1939–1975* (New York: Random House, 1980), 93.

[2] Weinstein and Vassiliev, *Haunted Wood*, 198.

[3] Douglas, *Court Years*, 80.

[4] *Ibid.*

[5] *Ibid.*, 82.

[6] Rosa Parks, *My Story* (Reprint, Puffin Books, 1999), 63.

[7] *Ibid.*, 113.

[8] Mays, *Born to Rebel*, 199.

[9] *Ibid.*, 265.

[10] Parks, *My Story*, 138.

[11] Martin Luther King Jr., *The Autobiography of Martin Luther King, Jr.*, ed. by Claiborne Carson (Grand Central Publishing, 1998), 98.

[12] *Ibid.*, 67.

[13] *Ibid.*, 86.

[14] *Ibid.*, 82.

[15] Parks, *My Story*, 175.

[16] Haywood, *Black Communist*, 275.

[17] King, *Autobiography*, 20.

[18] *Ibid.*

[19] Mays, *Born to Rebel*, 308.

[20] *Ibid.*, 321.

EPILOGUE

[1] King, *Autobiography*, 122.

[2] Rowley, *Life and Times of Richard Wright*, 514.

[3] Ibid., 521.

[4] "Wealth Inequality Has Widened," Pew Research Center, Dec. 12, 2014, http://www.pewresearch.org/fact-tank/2014/12/12/racial-wealth-gaps-great-recession/.

[5] "Benjamin J. Davis, 60, Is Dead," *New York Times*, Aug. 24, 1964, 27.

[6] "Rusk's Daughter, 18, to Marry Negro," *New York Times*, Sept. 22, 1967, 1.

[7] Dolores Newton, interview with the author, Sept. 2012.

SELECTED WORKS

Burns, Robert. *I Am a Fugitive from a Georgia Chain Gang!* Athens: University of Georgia Press, 1997.

Carter, Dan T. *Scottsboro: A Tragedy of the American South.* Rev. ed. Baton Rouge: Louisiana State University Press, 1979.

Davis, Benjamin J. *Communist Councilman from Harlem.* International Publishers Co., 1969.

Douglas, William O. *The Court Years: 1939–1975.* New York: Random House, 1980.

Gilmore, Glenda Elizabeth. *Defying Dixie.* New York: W. W. Norton, 2008.

Haywood, Harry. *Black Communist in the Freedom Struggle: The Life of Harry Haywood.* Edited by Gwendolyn Midlo Hall. Reprint, Minneapolis: University of Minnesota Press, 2012.

Herndon, Angelo. *Let Me Live.* Arno Press and *New York Times*, 1969.

Jelks, Randal Maurice. *Schoolmaster of the Movement.* Chapel Hill: University of North Carolina Press, 2012.

King, Martin Luther, Jr. *The Autobiography of Martin Luther King, Jr.* Edited by Claiborne Carson. Grand Central Publishing, 1998.

Martin, Charles H. *The Angelo Herndon Case and Southern Justice.* Baton Rouge: Louisiana State University Press, 1976.

Mays, Benjamin. *Born to Rebel.* Athens: University of Georgia Press, 1971.

Parks, Rosa. *My Story.* Reprint, Puffin Books, 1999.

Pennyback, Susan D. *From Scottsboro to Munich: Race and Political Culture in 1930s Britain.* Princeton: Princeton University Press, 2009.

Robinson, Robert. *Black on Red*. Acropolis, 1988.

Rowley, Hazel. *The Life and Times of Richard Wright*. Chicago: University of Chicago Press, 2001.

Ryan, James G. *Earl Browder: The Failure of American Communism*. 2nd ed. Tuscaloosa: University of Alabama Press, 1997.

Seager, Allan. "Actress with Red Garters." In *Frieze of Girls: Memoirs as Fiction*. Ann Arbor: University of Michigan Press, 2004.

Weinstein, Allen, and Alexander Vassiliev. *The Haunted Wood*. New York: Random House, 1999.

Woodward, Emily. *Empire: Georgia Today in Pictures and Paragraphs*. Atlanta: Ruralist Press, 1936.

Wright, Richard. *Black Boy*. Reprint, First Perennial Classics, 1998. First published in 1945 by Harper & Brothers.

———. *Native Son*. New York: Harper & Brothers, 1940.

INDEX

"Hoovervilles," 34-35
Hotel Russischer Hof, 27
Houston, TX, 9, 10, 11
Howard University School of Religion, 38, 96
Howe, Emmett, 119-20
Hudson, John, 65
Huntsville, AL, 49

Illinois Emergency Relief Commission, 52, 92
International Labor Defense, 42, 49, 50, 62, 76, 80, 82, 100, 120
International Negro Committee, 91

Jackson, Carrie, 60
Jan (*Native Son* character), 107-8
Jefferson School of Social Sciences, 121
John Reed Club, 74-75, 85
Johnson, Alex, 24
Jones, Dewey, 80
Jonesboro, AR, 10

Kennedy administration, 3
King, Coretta, 142
King, Martin Luther Jr., 134, 135-36, 137, 138-40, 142-43, 145
King, Martin Luther Sr., 134
Kirsanova, Klavdiia, 35
Klarin, Julius, 41
Klarin, Lizette, 41
Kling, Jack, 83-84

Knoch, Win G., 81
Kreisler, Fritz, 12
Ku Klux Klan, 2, 24, 39
Kuh, Sydney, 81
KUTV, 26, 27-32, 47, 93, 94, 122

La Guardia, Fiorello, 119
Law, Oliver, 89, 94
Learner, Aaron, 81
LeCraw, Roy, 64, 65
Left Front, 75
Leibowitz, Samuel, 50, 100-101
Lenin School, 31, 32, 34, 126
Lenin, Vladimir, 20, 24
Levin, Meyer, 85
Liberator, The, 34, 41, 44
Licht, Mary, 39-40, 41, 42, 43, 46, 105
Longworth, Nicholas, 47
Lonsdale, Frederick, 47
Los Alamos National Laboratory, 130
Louis, Joe, 88-89
Lysacht, William W., 48

MacArthur, Douglas, 12
Malraux, André, 111
Man's Hope, 111
Manhattan Project, 130
Martha's Vineyard, 115
Marx, Karl, 20, 49, 139-40
Mason, Elaine, 112
Mays, Benjamin, 22, 23, 24, 37, 38, 52, 96, 97, 134, 135, 137, 140-41
Mays, Benjamin's mother, 38